THE AMERICAN NETHERLANDER

THE AMERICAN NETHERLANDER

25 YEARS OF EXPAT TALES

Greg Shapiro

XPM
SINCE 1999

Published by XPat Media, Van Boetzelaerlaan 153, 2581 AR, The Hague, the Netherlands
Tel.: +31(0)70 306 33 10 – E-mail: info@xpat.nl – Internet: www.xpatmedia.nl

COVER ILLUSTRATION Floor de Goede
BACK COVER PHOTO Adrie Mouthaan
DESIGN Bram Vandenberge
CARTOONS Floor de Goede
PHOTOGRAPHS The author
FINAL EDITING Stephanie Dijkstra
PRINTING DZS grafik
DISTRIBUTION www.scriptum.nl

ISBN 978 94 6319 226 2 | NUR 740

www.xpat.nl
www.howtobeorange.nl
www.gregshapiro.nl

This book is a work of non-fiction, based on the life, experiences and recollections of the author. The author reserves the right to adapt or streamline details for the sake of privacy or expediency. Quotes, events and details are not a reliable source of journalistic accuracy; rather, they are subjective tools used to tell a story. The author has stated to the publisher that, while certain details may have been changed, the essential details are based on true experience. Portions of the text have appeared in stage shows at Boom Chicago Comedy Theater, as blog pieces on Dutchnews.nl, and in The XPat Journal. The author extends his gratitude for the help he received in developing the material.

INTRODUCTION

The American Netherlander is an anthology of my first two books. *How to Be Orange: an Alternative Dutch Assimilation Course* was inspired by my solo theater show. And *How to Be Dutch: The Quiz* was a collection of all the questions I thought *should* be included in the actual Dutch citizenship exam. By now, both printings have sold out, thank you very much. And since I'm celebrating 25 years in the Netherlands, I thought I'd do a rewrite of both books and include them in one volume.

If you're looking for an official guide to Dutch culture, this is not it. If you're looking for one man's completely subjective and utterly biased impression of Dutch culture, then you have come to the right place.

FOR INEZ

TABLE OF CONTENTS

PART TWO – THE QUIZ

PART ONE

PROLOGUE

Celebrating 25 Years in ~~Holland~~... sorry, *the Netherlands*

I came to the Netherlands in 1994 to take a job for just one summer. Twenty-five years later, I'm still here. So, fair warning: the Dutch can be addictive. I suppose I am the classic definition of an expat. I grew up in one country, I moved to another country, and I stopped. I came here thinking, "Nice country. Shame about the language..." But I stayed anyway. I came for work, I stayed for love, and – when I have to – I speak the language called *Dunglish*.

I happen to live in Amsterdam, and a lot of this book takes place there. But I've spent time in all corners of the Netherlands, from Den Bosch to Den Helder, from Limburg to Leeuwarden, from Scheveningen to Schiermonnikoog. And I love it all! (Except Kerkdriel, sorry.) The fact is there are 12 provinces in the Netherlands, and 10 don't have *Holland* in the title. This gets pointed out within 1.5 seconds, when you perform a show in, say, Eindhoven. "Hello, Holland" quickly results in "Ja, hallo! This is Brabant!" I even had trouble when I performed in Friesland. I said, "Friesland is my new favorite province," and someone yelled: "It's not a province! This is an occupied territory!" (Don't mess with Friesland).

When I got here, the country couldn't make up its mind what to call iself. Interestingly, neither could I. Growing up, my name was *Greg Shore*. That was my step-father's name. But it was Dutch folks who

would interrogate me about my authentic name: "What's your birth name? Shapiro? Then THAT'S your name!" I grew up thinking *Shapiro* sounded too ethnic, too Jewish. But Dutch people I encountered universally replied, "*Shapiro*: cool name." What better way to say, "Welcome?" And my name was not the only one that would change.

When I came to the Netherlands, the country marketing said 'Visit Holland.' The logo of the tourism board was a tulip saying 'Welcome to Holland.' And the in-flight KLM magazine was called *The Holland Herald*. It's no wonder most people fail to realize the name of the country is *the Netherlands*. Maybe it's just too long, too clunky, not great for marketing. But then came a little viral video called 'Netherlands Second,' which turned out to be pretty good advertising for this country's true name. Soon after that, came *the Netherlands winning Eurovision!*

And now – for the first time in at least 25 years – the Dutch government is ditching the term *Holland* from all official correspondence and rebranding as *the Netherlands*.

You're welcome.

CHAPTER 1
AMSTERDAM DAY ONE

"Look at our legs! Look at our legs!"

– The Amsterdam Welcoming Committee

The question was: "Would you be willing to give up your acting career in Manhattan to do comedy in Amsterdam for a start-up theater called *Boom Chicago*?" Since I was living on tips and paying rent via credit card, the answer was an immediate YES. When you've tried being broke in New Amsterdam, you might as well try being broke in Old Amsterdam.

In 1994, my idea of Amsterdam was the one shared by most Americans, I suppose: Rembrandt, Van Gogh, Anne Frank – and then sex & drugs and downhill from there. In America, if we hear about the Netherlands at all, it's that Dutch people are all drug-doing, drug-dealing, baby-killing, grandpa-murdering, left-handed pedophiles. Once I got here, I realized it's not true! According to most Dutch people: "That's Belgium."

I remember getting off the plane at Schiphol Airport and thinking there must have been a mistake. It was such a modern, sleek, well-designed airport. And the baggage carts were actually larger – LARGER! – than their American counterparts. Not to mention they were free of charge. I had seriously misjudged the Netherlands. The signs were in English. The ads were for Samsonite. And the first thing I saw out of Customs was a Burger King. I thought I was in Pittsburgh.

And the charm offensive continued. Instead of having to surrender my baggage cart, I was able to take it right down to the train platform. It was my first time on a walkway escalator, and the handbrake on my baggage cart actually worked. Within one hour, I'd already started to redefine my definition of *Second-World Country.* That term was now reserved for JFK International in New York.

Before leaving Schiphol Airport, I took care of my To-Do List of Now-Anachronistic technology. I went to a place called the GWK Currency Exchange to trade my US Dollars into a totally made-up currency called *Guilders.* Even at the time, Guilders seemed whimsically antiquated. One of the coins they gave me said '2-and-a-half.' I supposed it was from back in the days when people counted on their two-and-a-half fingers. I also bought a public transport pass called a 'strip card,' since access to Dutch trams somehow involved 'stripping.' The alternative was 'Riding Black' – which to me sounded like a stripper name. And lastly, I procured a phone card for making phone calls at these things called 'public phone booths.' These triangular, glass enclosures were also known as 'phone boxes,' or – in Dutch – *pissoirs.*

CULTURE SHOCK

From the modern Schiphol Airport, I then took the train into Amsterdam Centraal Station, and there it was! The rundown former glory I'd been expecting. Stepping out of the train, I quickly realized the smoking section was 'Everywhere.' The smell of cannabis was not limited to the coffeeshops. And – instead of ferry boats on the water side of the station – there was a veritable junkie wasteland. Nowadays, on the water side, there are dedicated bike lanes and harbor-side cafés. In 1994, there was a busy road, urine-soaked concrete, and a waterfront no-man's-land. Locals deemed it "too dangerous even to buy a junkie bike." In the train pulling into Amsterdam CS, you could look down and see prostitutes performing live sex shows, and junkies shooting up. It was an urban Garden of Earthly Delights – the Amsterdam version of Hieronymus (from Den Bosch) Bosch.

After exiting the station on the Amsterdam Centrum side, I had to dodge a team of hotel hawkers. Hotel hawkers were from the era when hotels thought the best way to make a first impression was with shaggy, unwashed stoners pitching to tourists as they came out of the station. After the hawkers, came the Damrak. The Damrak circa 1994 was a messy barrage of tacky signs for tourist-trap shops, made worse by barricades from complicated street construction. So, basically the same as ever.

Outside Centraal Station, I remember my real first impression was the bikes. I had never seen so many bicycles in one place! It seemed like there were more bikes than people. …And that was 100% accurate. It still is. We don't know how the bikes are repopulating. Government officials are constantly trying to thin the herd.

And then there were the people *riding* the bikes: they were so tall! I'd spent most of my life being the tallest one around. Now maybe I could feel more at home. And specifically, I was noticing the *women* riding the bikes. Was it me, or were they showing a LOT of leg?

I didn't realize it at the time, but it was the 4th of April and the first really warm day of the year – an occasion which is now known unofficially as *Rokjesdag*. 'Short skirt day.' The day that Dutch women collectively look in their closets and decide, "Yes. I'm going with the short skirt." For me, it was like a kick-line parade of Dutch legs saying, "Welcome! Welcome to Amsterdam!" How could I not stay?

CHAPTER 2

BOOM CHICAGO EARLY DAYS

"The *Zwarte Piet* Revolution is about to begin."

– Jordan Peele & Colton Dunn in 'Zwarte Piet Rap,' 2002

The very first year Boom Chicago comedy theater performed in Amsterdam, the rehearsal space was under a bridge next to Central Station. I'm glad I came the second year.

Boom Chicago was founded by two friends of mine from school: Andrew & Pep. Here's how they describe their origin story:

> "Americans Pep Rosenfeld and Andrew Moskos graduated from university and were traveling in Europe. They were sampling some local Amsterdam culture on the Leidseplein, and they had what they claim is 'the best stoner idea ever': quit their jobs in the U.S. and move permanently to Amsterdam to start a comedy show. The reason they picked Amsterdam is not what you think… It was the drugs.
>
> They wrote the Amsterdam Board of Tourism for some advice, and the VVV wrote back very quickly: 'Your idea will not work.' The letter went on: 'Dutch People do not want to see a show in English. Tourists do not want to see a show at all. You will need subsidy to do theater in the Netherlands. You will not get any subsidy.' (Well, they were right about that one.)"

In 1994, there wasn't much pay. Boom Chicago compensated us primarily with airfare, housing and meals. And a bike. A junkie bike. In 1994, it was not uncommon to be approached by someone late at night saying, "*Fiets te koop!*" Bike for sale! The going rate for a good bike was about 50 Guilders. Soon, I found myself wandering a dark street on the way home from work, with 50 Guilders in my pocket.

It was near the Red Light District that I found a thoroughly disreputable-looking gentleman on a bike, saying, "Wanna buy?" I nodded yes and followed him into one of the myriad shadowy corners. I looked at the bike. It seemed rather new. I asked, "How much?" He said, "25 Guilders." I held up my money and asked, "Can I try it first?" Now nervous, the man said, "Yeah. Here." He gave me a small plastic bag. Then he took my money, hopped on the bike and took off. Like an idiot, I followed him, saying, "You forgot your bag..."

A quick examination of the plastic baggie proved that I hadn't purchased a bike at all, but instead what looked like crack cocaine. It's possible I'd purchased crack. More likely was I'd encountered an Amsterdam tradition: fake drug dealers. At this point I'd drawn a bit of attention to myself, since I was holding up a bag of drugs in the street. Even in Amsterdam this can draw attention. One downtrodden guy was looking at me curiously. I said, "Can you believe it? I was trying to buy the bike. Instead, I got fake drugs." Wide-eyed, the guy said, "Let me see that..." The way he cherished the bag, I'd started to think maybe it wasn't fake. It occurred to me to say, "That'll be 25 Guilders, Sir..." But in retrospect, I was happy to get out of there with my syringe virginity.

Soon, I'd successfully acquired a bike, and I was rehearsing for the new show – indoors! We were preparing our unique mix of sketches and improv, writing material ripped from the headlines – meaning it's now hopelessly outdated. Remember when the Eurotunnel was new? We had a sketch about that. Remember when MTV was hot? We had a sketch about that. Remember when World Cup 1994 was in the US? No one does. In fact, even now, most people react to the US hosting the World Cup like Dutch people first reacted to Boom Chicago doing English-language improv comedy in Amsterdam: "Are you sure this is a good idea? People here have never heard of this thing you do. I mean sure, you *could* do it – but who would come?"

Luckily, Boom Chicago had a secret weapon: on-street promotion. By us. That was the rule: three hours of street promo for every two hours of show. Do you know those poor people who have to stand on busy shopping streets trying to bother you about charities or newspaper subscriptions? Well, we were lower than that. With no matching outfits, we were much closer to the sleazy hotel hawkers I mentioned in Chapter 1. The good news was we were giving out free Amsterdam tour guides, with a comedic twist – and a very favorable review of our show. We were meant to go after the tourists. Specifically, the English-speaking tourists. I learned pretty quickly how to spot them from a block away. *Invita* backpacks & tight-fitting clothes? Italian. Avoid them. Sporty, outdoor mountain-climbing gear and baggy jeans? Those were the Americans. Stag parties staggering in the gutter? Those were the Brits.

In 1994, Boom Chicago performed in a theater across from the Melkweg club. (Boom Chicago's 1993 shows were played in the Korte Leidsedwarsstraat at a salsa club that no longer exists.) In 1994, we did our trademark, Chicago-style mix of sketches and improv. We made pizzas. And we served beer in plastic pitchers – some of which had been liberated from the actual Second City theater back in Chicago. In the kitchen at one point, Boom Chicago employed a young man named Ruben van

der Meer. He learned a valuable lesson: if you get a chance to do improv on TV, do it in Dutch.

At one point, I got good at street promo. I used a secret weapon: bounce shoes. My boss had bought them, thinking they'd help with jumping. But the real advantage was speed. Part of the problem of on-street promo is timing. Sometimes you wait and wait for the right people, but when they show up, you're not positioned well. With the bounce shoes, I had a much bigger range. I could run 50 meters in about five seconds. Sometimes I'd make eye contact with people across the Leidseplein and they'd think they were safe from awkward physical contact. But then – boing! boing! boing! – I'd be handing them our comedy guide book. At one point, I took to wearing a cape. It was ridiculous fun.

If I'd have had a choice, I probably wouldn't have picked on-street promo. I'd much sooner have chosen 'Get Subsidy & Hire Promo.' But – in retrospect – I'm glad for all that experience. It was on-street promo that was my introduction to Dutch actor Peter Faber. It was on-street promo that had us performing for Jam Master Jay. And Pink. And Ron Jeremy. (Not all at the same show…) My colleague Rob was doing on-street promo when he met Burt Reynolds, who ended up visiting Boom Chicago and coming onstage to steal the show by responding to a heckle: "Why yes, this my real hair. You know how I know? Because I paid $5,000 for it."

BOOM ALUMNI

In the early '90s, there was a big bang of comedy in Amsterdam. First came Boom Chicago, then Comedy Cafe, then Comedy Train, then Comedy Explosion. In the early years, Boom Chicago would do the summer season and then go back to Chicago for the winter. That's when I'd remember "I hate Chicago winters." Soon enough I was dating a Dutch woman, and we were getting serious. Maybe she'd want to move with me to the States? We decided to book a trip to Chicago to meet my family. It was planned for the week between Christmas and New Year's Eve. Meaning her first impression of my home country was: winter in Chicago. She said, "I love you, but I hate this." We decided to stay in the Netherlands.

I made my decision to stay in the Netherlands at about the same time I started working with people who would go back to the US and do quite well. Here are some fun stories about a few of them.

SETH MEYERS AS CAPTAIN TECHNOLOGY

Seth Meyers was a few years behind me at Northwestern University, and when he came to Amsterdam he was already popular with the management because he could touch type. Seth was a script-writing machine. For every script we'd bring to rehearsal, he'd bring three. And his scripts quickly started showing influences of Amsterdam. During Queen's Day 1997, someone acquired an enormous, hand-made headdress from the *vrijmarkt*. Pretty soon Seth had written a sketch incorporating the headdress – about two FBI agents monitoring a cult leader who used this weird headdress to recruit people. It was not a script that did very well. But his quantity quickly led to quality. 1997 was the year *Saving Private Ryan* premiered, and Seth wrote a D-Day-themed sketch about stoner tourists trying to cross the Amsterdam tram tracks – and finding it as difficult as the Normandy invasion. This sketch ran onstage for years. But the scripts were only half the show! Then there was the improv.

Back when the internet was new, Boom Chicago invented an improv game with a character called Captain Technology. Together with his sidekick, he would take complicated, technical problems and make them simple. Here's the twist: the sidekick would be played by a volunteer from the audience. In developing the game, we needed a name for the sidekick. As a reminder to 'keep things simple,' we called the sidekick 'Kid Simple.' As Americans, we had no idea there was a double meaning.

The first few times we did 'Captain Technology' onstage, we got an American volunteer, and there was no problem. Volunteers onstage mostly played along and tried not to take too many chances. So imagine our surprise when we got a British guy onstage to play Kid Simple, and he made a character choice I'd describe as 'mildly retarded.'

Directly after the show, our British friends came up and explained: "In the UK, *simple* means *retarded*." Oops! But somehow, we still didn't change the name. The next night, we got a Dutch volunteer onstage. "I'm Captain Technology," said Seth. "And you're my sidekick Kid Simple!" The Dutch guy went on to play a sidekick who was part retarded, part deaf-mute and part spastic. He really committed. In a horrendous way, it was – to us – hilarious. Leave it to the Dutch guy to be the most politically incorrect.

PETE GROSZ AND THE JUNKIE BIKE

Pete came over with Seth Meyers in 1997. And yes, the junkie bike market was still alive and well. At one point the newspapers started reporting on it. And a Boom Chicago colleague was caught on camera. On the front page of Amsterdam's newspaper *Het Parool*. They were doing an exposé on the rampant sale of junkie bikes in Amsterdam, and they had a tryptic of photos chronicling the sale, with the faces blurred. But to anyone who knew him, it was obvious: that man was our colleague 'Peter G.' The location was right next to Boom Chicago in the Korte Leidsedwarsstraat. Boom Chicago was not implicated, but we enjoyed referring to Pete as 'Peter G.'

AMBER RUFFIN AS THE BOSS

Amber first came over in 2004, and by then Boom Chicago actors were performing for lots of corporate events. With corporate events in our own theater, we'd have a certain amount of control. But with corporate events on location, the situation would frequently get out of control. And right from the start, Amber would respond with her trademark over-enthusiasm.

For corporate events on location, we used to rotate the job of corporate Contact Person. We rotated in and out of each other's roles in casting our shows, so it seemed logical to rotate the role of Contact Person as well. Anyway, it seemed logical to us. But pretty soon, we noticed a discernible difference in the way corporate clients reacted to me – a tall, white, male – and our female colleagues. Or our Black and female colleagues.

There was once a series of corporate events we did for a telephone guide. To convince the world they still needed a telephone guide. (It didn't work.) On that show, as it happened, Amber was Contact Person. She'd made contact with the client by phone before the show, she'd coordinated our arrival time, and she'd said, "See you there." When we got there – sure enough – the client did not see her. Instead, he made eye contact with me, the tall white man: "Would you like to see the stage?" I looked straight at Amber and said. "Gee. I don't know… Let me check with your Contact Person!" It wasn't the first time this had happened, and I enjoyed every time deferring to Amber, who was – on location – my boss.

Most times, the client would shake it off and turn to Amber and say, "Oh, *you're* Amber! We spoke by phone." But the telephone guide guy could not make the cognitive leap. He looked from me to my colleague Tarik, a Black man. "Are you the one I spoke to by phone?" No. "It was Amber." Then it dawned on him – for that brief moment – to talk to Amber. But for the rest of the day, he kept referring his questions to me. I kept having to say, "Let me check with my boss." It was super annoying.

And now I can almost imagine how Amber must feel being Black and female. But what I can't imagine is how she always manages to bounce back. In this case, she made a joke out of the situation by creating a new secret nickname for our client: ScrunchFace. "Because some poor people are born with a face that everybody wants to scrunch."

IKE BARINHOLTZ AND THE PULL

Ike Barinholtz came to Amsterdam in 1999. Onstage, he was known for playing the macho, likable doofus. Offstage, he was mostly a macho, likable doofus. Ike was the one who introduced real-life Fight Club to the Late Night improv show, in which Joe Canale would make jokes about Ike, and Ike would try to for-real punch Joe in the face. Ike was the one who put on a special, backstage show once he discovered that farts were flammable. And Ike had pull. It was like – for every new Dutch drug he discovered – his body invented a new pheromone the Netherlands had never smelled before.

Ike is a *mensch*. He was at my wedding, and he was around when my little daughter was born. Flash forward to the Boom Chicago 25th anniversary, and my daughter was now turning 18! Ike couldn't believe it. At the afterparty, I saw my wife talking to the Meyers family, my son was talking to Amber, and my daughter was talking to Ike. Part of me had to think back to Ike's legendary pull, and I had a small heart attack: "Does he know she's not yet 18?!"

But in fact, what I was witnessing was my daughter asking Ike what it's like to work with Zac Efron. Ike replied, "Gee, I don't know. Let's ask him right now." And he texted with Zac while my daughter watched. Ike typed, "I'm here in Amsterdam, where this girl wants to marry you." Zac texted back, "Awesome! Tell her I say hi." And is my daughter still blushing? Ha! Bet on it.

JORDAN PEELE AND ZWARTE PIET

Jordan started his comedy career in Amsterdam in 2001. He was so young! By now Jordan has won an Oscar – Best Original Screenplay for the 2016 film *Get Out*. And now I'm wondering how much inspiration he might have gotten from his time in Amsterdam. At this point, it would be easy to make the joke that Jordan might have gotten inspiration from the amount of weed he smoked while he was here. So yes, I'll make that joke. Jordan smoked so much weed he was like Cinderella: every night at midnight he'd transform after 12 bongs.

A quick story about the weed: In 2002, Boom Chicago did a stage swap with Second City theater in Chicago. In fact, that was where Jordan first met Keegan-Michael Key, at the improv set after the shows. Boom Chicago wanted to bring all our tech gear for video and effects, because Second City didn't have that stuff then. In 2003, that meant each of us actors had to bring one check in bag with clothes – and one extra check in bag with tech items like beamer, video board, or signal splitter.

And then came the moment that Jordan Peele gave us his classic recipe for how to sleep on the flight: weed. We all went outside – that was the smoking section then. Jordan said he'd got this strong indica stuff, "and it's guaranteed to knock you out once you get in the plane." Or *before* we got in the plane, as it turned out. Pep Rosenfeld and I were together, both developing a kind of paranoid high – right in time for the security check. And this was right after 9/11, so they had these interrogation stations set up before you'd even get to security. Sure enough, the first thing they asked was: "Did you pack your bags yourself?" And for the first time ever, the answer was actually NO. We did our best to bluff our way through, but both of us were sweating bullets. And the agent said, "You look rather nervous. Anything you'd like to tell me?" And that's when Pep confessed: "Our colleague gave us some weed in the smoking section outside, and it was pretty strong." And so we learned a valuable lesson that day: your weed tolerance will never compete with that of Jordan Peele.

Back to *Get Out*. In the film, Jordan Peele's main character Chris is invited to leave his home, go visit a bunch of white people, and feel like he's onstage the whole time. That pretty much sums up Jordan's life in Amsterdam. Was Jordan the token Black guy? Apparently, he thought so. In 2002, Boom Chicago hired Colton Dunn, also African American. Jordan later revealed that he was afraid for his job, assuming that no comedy group would want two Black guys in the ensemble at the same time.

In the film *Get Out*, the bad guys aren't overt racists – in fact, they're *progressives*. And Dutch culture is famously progressive – tolerant, open and multi-ethnic. Making it all the more jarring when you encounter *Zwarte Piet* for the first time – which Jordan did in 2001. I watched as Jordan's mouth fell open in stunned silence. (More on that in Chapter 13.) And I watched as Dutch folks prided themselves for being tolerant and culturally aware – while putting on blackface and saying, "This isn't offensive." It may have been the inspiration for Bradley Whitford saying he'd have voted for Barack Obama a third time – before strapping on his brain surgery gear.

There's a poster for *Get Out* with the tagline: 'Just because you're invited doesn't mean you're welcome.' Oddly enough, at the same time Jordan was winning his Oscar, the Dutch Prime Minister was running a campaign ad called 'Celebrating Sinterklaas Doesn't Make You Racist.' It was also in that campaign that the Prime Minister published an open letter to immigrants in the Netherlands, with the phrase 'If you don't like it here – GET OUT.'

SO there you have it, Nederland! You can claim partial credit for Jordan Peele's Oscar. All you have to do is admit that some people really do experience blackface as a little bit offensive.

CHAPTER 3

PULP FICTION
The Rewrite

"You know what the funniest thing about Europe is? It's the little differences. I mean, they got the same shit over there that we got here, but it's just... there, it's a little different."

– Quentin Tarantino via John Travolta

For many English-speakers around the world, it's like, "Everything I needed to know about Amsterdam I learned from that scene in *Pulp Fiction*." John Travolta and Samuel L. Jackson talking about the 'Hash bars,' the cops in Amsterdam, and *frites* with mayonnaise. ("Eww!")

I still remember the thrill of watching *Pulp Fiction* in 1994, at the Kriterion cinema – and the Sneak Preview. For the Boom Chicago crew, Tuesday night was Sneak Preview night. In the Netherlands, films would premiere on a Wednesday – meaning the actual film reels in canisters would have to be delivered to the cinemas to be premiered. If the film reels arrived a day early, that's what they'd show for the Tuesday Sneak Preview. Sometimes it would be a Danish film with Dutch subtitles, and we'd be out of luck. But sometimes it would be *The Fugitive* – with Dutch actor Jeroen Krabbé. Not too shabbé!

So imagine our surprise when the sneak preview was not only the much-hyped *Pulp Fiction*, as we'd been hoping – but there was an entire scene about life in Amsterdam! We were there watching John Travolta on the big screen, saying, "You can walk into a movie theater in Amsterdam and buy a beer. And I don't mean just like no paper cup. I'm talking about a glass of beer." And there I was in a movie theater in Amsterdam – with a glass of beer! It was like, "He's talking to *me*!"

I watched *Pulp Fiction* again recently, and I realized there is new meaning to that quote about the 'little differences.' Those little differences between the US and Europe are now pretty big differences. But even bigger are the differences between the Netherlands in 1994 and the Netherlands now. In fact, if Quentin Tarantino were to remake *Pulp Fiction* today, the dialogue would have to be quite different.

For example:
1994: "So tell me again about the hash bars in Amsterdam."
Hash bars? No. Coffeeshops? Yes.

Rewrite: "So tell me again about the *coffeeshops* in Amsterdam."
In Amsterdam, hash bars are called *coffeeshops*. Why? Because in the late 1960s, there was a certain café with a certain regular patron who was certain to sell you marijuana – if you knew to ask for the 'coffeeshop.' [The original coffeeshop was called Mellow Yellow, and it was forced to close in 2017.] The police announced they were okay with the 'coffeeshop' plan. And soon after came a series of cafes known as coffeeshops, i.e. hash bars. (The fact they chose an English-language term makes me think that first customer was definitely British.)

Legend has it Tarantino used the term *coffeeshop* in his first draft of *Pulp Fiction*, but Americans were so confused he had to change it to 'hash bar.' Meanwhile, American terminology is not much clearer. In America, a common term for pharmacy is *drug store*. And in Amsterdam – when tourists ask for the 'drug store' – you can watch as they are directed to the coffeeshop.

1994: "You can't just go into a restaurant and start puffing away... They want you to smoke it in your home or certain designated places."

Sorry, *Pulp Fiction*. Since 2007, Dutch non-smoking laws include restaurants – as well as the 'certain designated places' known as coffeeshops. If *Pulp Fiction* were remade today, the dialogue would have to be a little different.

Rewrite:

Travolta: "...They want you to smoke it in your home or certain designated places."

Jackson: "And the designated places are called coffeeshops?"

Travolta: "Technically, the designated places are the smoking rooms inside the coffeeshops."

Jackson: "You can't smoke inside the coffeeshop?"

Travolta: "The only way you can smoke is if they have a smoking area."

Jackson: "A smoking area?!"

Travolta: "Yeah, you know. A specially constructed, hermetically sealed smoking area inside the coffeeshop, to protect all the people who don't smoke."

Jackson: "WHAT ARE YOU DOING IN A COFFEESHOP IF YOU DON'T SMOKE?"

1994: "Hash is legal, but it ain't 100% legal."

In fact, hash is technically 100% illegal. But Dutch police chose to decriminalize marijuana since it's a 'soft drug.'

Rewrite:

Travolta: "Hash has never been legal, it's just that soft drugs are tolerated."

Jackson: "Soft drugs – like mushrooms?"

Travolta: "Not exactly... Since 2008, you can get some kinds of mushrooms, but not the good ones like dried mushrooms."

Jackson: "What if I buy the mushrooms and dry them myself?"

Travolta: "No one does that. Because all you gotta do is ask for 'truffles.'"

1994: "Get a load of this. If the cops stop you in Amsterdam, it's illegal for them to search you. That's a right the cops actually don't have."

Rewrite:
Travolta: "Yeah, it's different since 2001. After 9/11, the cops can now search you whenever they want."

Jackson: "Damn!"

Travolta: "And if they search you, you'd better have valid ID – with your government-approved photo on it. Otherwise you can be arrested. It's like back in Germany. You must have your papers, *und* your papers must be correct at all times!"

1994: 'It breaks down like this: it's legal to buy it, it's legal to own it... And – if you're the proprietor of a hash bar – it's legal to sell it.'

Rewrite:
Travolta: "If you're the proprietor of a hash bar, it's legal to sell it... but since 2012, it's only legal to sell it if your coffeeshop is beyond 250 meters of a school."

Jackson: "What if it's not?"

Travolta: "Then they'll shut you down like they did the first-ever coffeeshop, Mellow Yellow."

Jackson: "Because it was too close to a school?"

Travolta: "Well, the school is actually now a health club, so no one knows why. But also – your coffeeshop can't be too close to the border with Belgium. And also – you have to check the passports of all your clientele to make sure there are no tourists."

Jackson: "No tourists? Who exactly is smoking this hash?"

Travolta: "Mostly tourists."

Jackson: “Why would you need to keep the people out of the hash bar, who are the only people who want to go into the hash bar?”

Travolta: “Don’t ask me! But it’s still legal to buy it, it’s legal to own it…”

Jackson: “Is it legal to grow it?”

Travolta: “No.”

Jackson: “Where does the hash come from then?!”

Travolta: “I don’t know! Hash fairies?”

Jackson: “Man, I don’t know who is coming up with these rules – but they have GOT to be smoking something.”

CHAPTER 4
MND
Multiple Nationality Disorder

"Travel is fatal to prejudice, bigotry, and narrow-mindedness"

– Mark Twain
(though he still used the N-word quite a bit)

When you spend time living abroad, there comes a moment when you go back home – and you get culture shock. *In your home country*. If you've ever lived outside the country where you grew up – as many Dutch folks have – then you could be living with a condition I call MND: Multiple Nationality Disorder. See if any of these MND symptoms sound familiar.

FOOD

I grew up in America with a dessert called 'Dutch Apple Pie.' It was nothing like the real Dutch apple pie. The American recipe involved sticky, grey, apple-flavored glucose goo. When I came to the Netherlands and ordered apple pie, I tasted real chunks of apple and a real butter crust. Enlightened, I took the recipe back to the US. Proudly, I presented it to my friends and family – and they were disappointed. They said, "It's good, but it's not quite *Dutch Apple Pie*."

FACES

I'd been living abroad for over a year, and I flew back home with a layover. As I sat at the airport people-watching, I realized: "These people look *foreign.*" Had they all changed since I'd been away? In particular, everyone's eyeglasses looked huge. Had America developed some new trend while I'd been gone? ...And then I realized: nothing in America had changed. The only thing that had changed was my perception of what standard eyewear should look like, based on the tiny little reading glasses that Dutch people call 'normal.'

It's no wonder a Dutchman invented the microscope. Ever since then – when it comes to eyewear – Dutch people seem to think: "It's a tiny country! We wouldn't want to see too much of it at any one time."

FASHION

I went back to the States and met some friends at a bar. They started teasing me for dressing like a 'Euro-pimp.' Why? Because I was wearing 'skinny jeans' – and clothes that were tailored to fit my body. I looked around, and they were all wearing the same version of mismatched outfits: athletic footwear, coupled with loose-fit jeans and t-shirts. The sneakers were saying: "I'm going to the gym!" But the rest was saying: "No, he's not."

Some people have split personalities – I have split nationalities. When you no longer feel completely at home anywhere, that's MND. This book is for you.

GAY!

CHAPTER 5
NEDERLANDS SECOND English First

"Do we need a translation into Dutch? Nah..."

– My publisher

It was a Thursday when I got the call from Janine Abbring at *Zondag Met Lubach*. She said, "Donald Trump is being sworn in as President tomorrow. Would you like to do your Trump voice for this video we're making?" I said, "So fantastic. I'd be totally great. BIGLY." They sent me the script. It said, "Grab 'em by the Pony." And I thought, "Oooh... This could be good."

The official title of the video from 2017 was 'The Netherlands Welcomes President Trump in his Own Terms.' But it quickly became known as 'The Netherlands Second' video. And this thing went so viral – back when 'viral' was a good thing. It went around the world and back. People were sending me the link from America, saying, "Have you seen this? You would love this!" And I said, "Yeah, mom... that's me."

Since then, people keep asking, "Do you think Trump himself has seen it?" And the answer is: I don't know. But I do know this. This video from the little Netherlands now has more views on YouTube than the official Trump inauguration video. So congratulations, Nederland. *Tjakka*!

NO ENGLISH PLEASE, WE'RE DUTCH

When I first arrived in 1994, there were not as many signs in English. Yes,

Dutch folks were watching *Friends* and Michael Jordan, but the cultural phenomenon known as 'The Internet' hadn't yet taken over. These days – between the Ice Bakeries and Amsterdam Cheese Companies – it can be hard to find signs in Dutch. In 1994, the billboards, the product labels, the basic city signage – it was all '*Nederlands* First! English Second.'

By the mid-90s, I started getting work in Dutch TV & film productions. If there was ever a Dutch production needing an English-speaking character, I'd sometimes get the call. I started out with a bit part in *Zonnetje in Huis*. By now, I've played a music producer in *Oh, Baby;* a catty modeling coach in *Radeloos;* and a news reader in *Phileine Zegt Sorry*. One of my favorite gigs was for the old-school soap opera *Goede Tijden Slechte Tijden, GTST*. In one of the story lines, the young love interest goes on a ski holiday and injures herself. Who plays the doctor? Me.

When I got to the set for *GTST* I said, "It's an American doctor, right?"
"No. He has to be French," was the answer.
"But the lines are in English."
"Well, just say them with a French accent," they said.

And there I was, on the set with Barbara and her daughter Charlie (Charlotte Besijn and Aukje van Ginneken). We were running our lines, and I wasn't sounding French enough. I tried a thicker accent. Again, the director asked, "More French, please." Just for fun, I did a crazy, broad French accent – like John Cleese in *Monty Python and the Holy Grail*. The director loved it. If you ever watch the clip back, you might be able to hear everyone on the set dying with laughter in the middle of the scene.

And then someone thought it would be a good idea to have me on the Big Film Quiz, *De Avond van de Grote Film Quiz*. Every year, Dutch public broadcasting would get a bunch of Dutch actors and make them compete in a number of challenges involving film trivia. Sometimes they'd have to identify film quotes, and sometimes they'd compete to do the best re-enactment of famous film scenes. And every year it was pretty fun. The host was Matthijs van Nieuwkerk from *De Wereld Draait Door* – the closest thing the Dutch had to *The Daily Show*.

I know Matthijs van Nieuwkerk from his days as director of Amsterdam broadcaster AT5. (It was there that we did the *Boom Chicago News* in 2001.) I know Matthijs speaks English, but at one point he'd made a rule for himself not to do it on TV. As he admitted in one of his last shows on air, it was the Andre Agassi interview. Apparently, the plan was for Matthijs to treat the guy like an intellectual and ask him his trademark, fast-paced questions. But Matthijs didn't feel 100% comfortable in English. And since that day, he made it a rule: "Only in my native language."

If only I had followed that rule. *The Big Film Quiz* was on Dutch public broadcasting. The producer asked me if I could speak Dutch on the show. The explanation was: "Unlike commercial television, the public broadcasters are aimed at, shall we say, *higher* educated viewers." Of course! It's that 'lowbrow' commercial programming that's filled with English language content – and expects the viewers to be multilingual. Pretty low education level, eh?

A producer from *De Wereld Draait Door* explained it to me. Like so many people, I came close to being interviewed on *De Wereld Draait Door* and got bumped last-minute. I teased the producer, saying, "I hear the public broadcasters have a secret 'No English' policy." She said, "No! ... It's not just English. It's any other language." She explained: "There's no written rule that Dutch public broadcasters have to stick to Dutch. But there's an unspoken rule that – if you're accepting money from the Dutch government – then you're expected to stick to the mother tongue."

Thus, Dutch public broadcasting acts as a sort of '*Academie Nederlandaise*.' "We're not chauvinistic! But we are protective of our *Nederlandse taal*." That's why I loved it when Matthijs van Nieuwkerk once invited guest-host Adriaan van Dis to take over the show for Book Week. Adriaan van Dis came on, and the first thing he did was switch languages. First came a fluent German interview, and then a fluent English interview. Three languages for the price of... well, less than Matthijs van Nieuwkerk.

OKAY, JUST A LITTLE ENGLISH

To their credit, many producers in Dutch public broadcasting have had no problem putting me and my English on TV. I was on *Jinek* in 2017, and host Eva Jinek said, "I speak English, the topic is in English, we're doing the interview in English. Why do we pay real-time translators, if we don't use them?" We did the interview in English. And I improvised, as Trump, in English. I said, "I'm not a religious man, but I do have an enormous messiah complex." It was English first, *Nederlands* second.

On BNRfm I did an Obama column with Bas van Werven, and we did it with questions in Dutch and answers in English. With Boom Chicago I've done so much English commentary. We appeared for Election 2016 on *Brandpunt*. I was with Pep Rosenfeld on *Twee voor Twaalf* in 2008. I spoke English for NOS Election Night in 2000 with Boom Chicago. And in 2004 – the same night that Theo van Gogh was murdered – Pep & I were in Hilversum for US election coverage on *Barend en van Dorp*. That was one of the most surreal experiences of my life. One dressing room was filled with Dutch politicians and commentators in shock; the other was filled with the obligatory popcorn and brownies and American football cheerleaders waving pom-poms. It was like *US Election Night* directed by David Lynch.

Back to *The Big Film Quiz*. The producer wanted me to play the character of a Hollywood reporter – but in Dutch. I asked if it might be a bit more believable if I spoke mostly English, with a little bit of Dutch thrown in. He said yes. Here's the script they gave me.

"Mijn naam is Greg Shapiro *van* The Hollywood Reporter *en ik ben hier bij de Avond van de Grote Filmquiz. We verwachten hier* anytime *de limousines met de sterren van de avond…"*

Just a little bit of Dutch.

The concept was not only for me to introduce the show. I was also to provide a through-line to the wacky ending. Every year on *The Big Film Quiz*, they ended the show with something unique. One year it was a *Full Monty* tribute where all the guys did a striptease. This year the plan was an ode to the classic American Pie Fight. The plan was that I would get steadily drunker on champagne during the show. And then – when they'd bring out the big birthday cake, I'd say something naughty and get hit in the face with cake.

Here's what happened in reality. First of all, I did the intro in broken Dutch. I said hello to Thomas Acda, Daniël Boissevain, Frank Lammers, De Meisjes van Toren C, and Johnny de Mol. They walked from the limo to the theater – and walked all over me. In the studio I was given an earpiece, which was a lot like experiencing schizophrenia: I was hearing voices, and they were all telling me different things.

The producer: "Go get a drink! We need to see you drinking champagne!"

The director: "Shapiro, what are you doing in the shot? Stop moving." You can watch the clip back on YouTube. While the script said they should cut back to me occasionally, the director skipped it. For most of the show, they don't have me in frame. So, at the end of the show – with no explanation at all – a drunken Shapiro comes onscreen. Out of nowhere I stagger into frame with trays full of enormous cakes.

The producer: "Cue Shapiro! Go Shapiro."

The director: "Shapiro, what are you doing?! Wait for Matthijs!"

I delivered the prizes, I presented the cakes, I waited for Matthijs.

The producer: "Start the Shapiro speech! "
The director: "What Shapiro speech?"

They told me to write up a little speech and make it so insulting the actors would really want to hit me with cake. It was now or never. Drunkenly, I said, "*Jullie Nederlanders zijn ZO bezig met elkaar*..." "You Dutch people are SO busy with yourselves. Dutch film festival, Golden Calf award, Edison award, Rembrandt award... 'Let's give each other more awards!' But meanwhile you don't have any Dutch films on the show tonight. All you talk about are American movies. All your clips are in English. Yet you make ME speak Dutch? You've all got your heads up your asses!"

And that's when Thomas Acda and sore loser Frank Lammers ignored me and started throwing cake at each other. Matthijs van Nieuwkerk had made it clear to everyone he did not want to be hit with any cake. No cake! ...It was Frank Lammers who walked over and put cake directly into Matthijs's hair. In the YouTube clip, you can see a chagrined Matthijs van Nieuwkerk, covered in cake and signing off, "We hope to see you next year..."

There would not be a next year.

CHAPTER 6

DUTCH IDENTITY
Who Are We?

"Is there one Dutch identity? I haven't found it... Nederland is too diverse to sum up in any one cliché."

– Máxima Zorreguieta, Queen of the Netherlands, originally from Argentina, 2009

"Máxima Says Dutch Identity Doesn't Exist."

- Dutch media, 2009

Not long after Máxima's infamous quote, I was invited to take part in a seminar on Dutch culture entitled 'Dutch Identity: Who Are We?' I was to join a panel discussion along with other internationals – and one Dutch guy. What happened next was fireworks.

The seminar started with a panel of elder Dutchmen. There was an expert on Dutch culture, a captain of Dutch industry, and a member of the Dutch government. The Dutch elders agreed that Máxima was wrong. There IS a Dutch identity. . . . But they couldn't agree on what it was, exactly. I remember thinking, "If you guys can't figure out the Dutch identity, who will?"

The first speaker said part of the Dutch identity is the need to disagree. Ever since they threw off Spanish Catholicism, the Dutch have celebrated their right to their own opinion – even if that means debating everything. In my experience, this is pretty true. When I introduced my mother to my Dutch family for the first time, and someone told her, "Nice outfit," it was my Dutch father-in-law who said, "I don't think so." And the debate was on! Next, we got to hear a lengthy monologue about everything wrong with American fashion. "All the sizes are too big. Everything has to be Loose-fit, Baggy-fit. But I understand that is to hide the fact that Americans are all so fat." While Dutch people have a reputation for being tolerant. But they're also judgmental as hell.

The second Dutch expert highlighted the Dutch as non-hierarchical. In a Dutch office, everyone wants to be their own boss. Except the actual boss, who spends time acting like they're NOT the boss and arriving by bike. He shared studies showing that the Netherlands is the least chauvinistic country in Europe. Note: not the most *modest* in Europe, but the least *chauvinistic*. If I'm performing for a Dutch audience, I'll sometimes ask, "How many Dutch people speak English pretty well?" The general response will be to stare at their shoes and say, "Meh..." But if

you change the question to "How many Dutch people speak English better than French people?" Wow! Just watch those hands shoot up. Maybe that's partly why the 'Netherlands Second' video was such a hit here. Dutch mentality is like, "We don't need to be first. But we are definitely better than the rest."

The third Dutch expert was a historian, who highlighted the Dutch as independent thinkers. During the Spanish Empire, the maps reached up to a certain point in the Netherlands and then stopped. But Dutch people kept building more and more land on the blue bits of the map. The Spanish said, "Cut it out." The Dutch said, "No." And that's part of the reason there was a revolution. (The Dutch Revolution is known as The 80 Years War. The reason it took 80 years is apparently because the Dutch were so non-hierarchical they couldn't make up their minds about anything.)

As far back as the Roman empire, the maps got as far as Utrecht and then gave up. But it was Dutch people who eventually settled the land beyond the frontier, in the swamp. Reclaiming land from the swamp is apparently an integral part of the Dutch collective identity. While the Scottish are known for saying, "Freedom!" – the Dutch were saying, "Get out of my swamp!" Historically speaking, Shrek should be orange.

Up next at the event was the panel. I was invited to sit onstage with a few expats – and an older Dutchman from Rabobank. Once Mr. Rabobank got the mic, he went off on a surprisingly passionate, anti-Dutch rant: "I've spent much of my career outside the Netherlands, and you should see how people look at us! You say we like to debate? I say we can never get anything done! You say we're not chauvinistic? Then why do people think we're so smug? You say we're non-hierarchical? I say we're a nation of followers! Our government is full of middle-management. Who will have the courage to stand up and lead?"

There was a question from the audience – specifically from the member of the Dutch government who'd spoken earlier. It seemed the two men knew each other. What followed next was a heated debate – while the rest of us in the panel looked at each other like, "Should we maybe leave the stage now?"

That's when the moderator stepped in to defuse the tension – by giving the mic to me. "Mr. Gregory Shapiro, you're a comedian. What's your opinion?" Gulp.

At that point, I must admit I had more questions than answers:

- *How can Dutch identity be so independent-minded, yet also so obsessed with consensus?*
- *How can Dutch identity be so liberal and open, yet also so Calvinistic & conformist?*
- *How can Dutch identity be so proud, but then be so quiet about it?*
- *More to the point: what on earth am I going to say to ease the obvious on-stage tension?*

I took the mic and referred back to the quote from Máxima. Máxima, who is an immigrant. And – whatever you may think of the Dutch on the world stage – the fact is that immigrants like it here. For me, it was inspiring to learn that so much of Dutch history was based on immigration. Indeed, some of the most famous Dutch names are imports: René Descartes, Baruch Spinoza, even William of Orange, who comes 'from German blood.'

So – while the elder Dutch white men would go on debating whether Dutch culture is worthy or not – there were new Dutch people from all over the world, who appreciate what Nederland stands for.

I realize there are many Dutch folks who worry about too many people coming to the Netherlands. Well, as an American, let me put it like this: If you don't want so many immigrants, then stop being so awesome.

CHAPTER 7
A WORD FROM Willem van Oranje

Hi, I'm William of Orange. You may know me as 'William the Silent.' But I cannot keep silent about this book! Yes, I was silent for a while about the atrocities of the Spanish Inquisition, but that was because I've always honored the King of Spain. That's How to be Dutch Lesson 1: Keep Spain happy. Spain will remain Europe's number one superpower for centuries to come.

It's not easy being Orange. Every time I say I'm proud to be from the 'United Provinces,' there's always someone reminding me I'm not really from here. They call me names, saying I'm actually from Nassouwe in Germany – or Orange in France. Well, now that I'm in charge I'll make sure we never make someone feel bad for where they came from. And we'll forever eliminate the word *allochtoon*.

If there's one thing I hope you take away from this book, it's this: long live the Republic! I gave everything I had to throw off the monarchy and to blaze a trail for a new system of government, based on self-rule. May we always have the right to self-determination, such as the right to directly elect our city mayors.

And if anyone told me this country would become a monarchy, I'd pull off my own mustache in rage. Or – at least if we ever do have a monarchy – I hope they'll have the good sense to avoid inbreeding and get some foreign blood into the mix.

– W. v. Oranje, Delft 1584

CHAPTER 8
DUTCH SEX LIFE
Culture Shock Therapy

'Durex ORGASMIC – Sex is fun!'

– Condom package on pharmacy checkout counter, at eye level.

Attitudes toward sex in the Netherlands can result in culture shock for many people. But if you spend a bit more time here, it becomes what I call Culture Shock Therapy. Yes, it's different than what you might be accustomed to, but then you realize: "This way is better!"

Dutch culture treats sex as a natural part of life, which is actually quite healthy. When I moved here in the '90s, I remember there was a Safe Sex outdoor campaign on posters and billboards. Since the subject was sex, the poster showed a naked couple – about to have sex. The image was this: a woman kneeling on her bed, topless. Standing in front of her: a big, Black dude, wearing nothing. With one hand, she's about ready to take off her undies, and with the other she's holding up a condom, saying, "*Doe jij iets aan, doe ik iets uit.*" "If you put something on, I'll take something off."

To me, it was the perfect way of saying, "You're not in America anymore." Granted, these days America has more sexually explicit imagery. And sometimes, there's even a little nudity. But both sexuality *and* nudity, combined with a Black guy in that white girl's bedroom? Many Americans would say, "Call the police!"

It gets awkward. I was once performing at a corporate event for an American company. The event was at a posh hotel on Amsterdam Dam Square, which is also right next to the Red Light District. The instructions were clear: yes, be interactive with the audience, but do NOT mention the Red Light District. So I asked the mostly male audience, "What you think of Amsterdam?" Unanimously, they answered, "The Red Light District!" I answered with a quick joke and moved on.

But the American organizer went berserk. She ran to the tech booth in back, trying simultaneously to wave me offstage and telling the technician to cut my mic. Luckily, the show went on, and it was fine! But afterward she was apoplectic with rage. She stammered, "You have killed a part of me… A part of me has died tonight." I was thinking, "I hope she doesn't see that AIDS poster."

The Red Light District has been described as an adult-themed outdoor amusement park. And – like most amusement parks – if you've been through it once, you pretty much get it. Every time I'm hosting people from back in the States, they want to see the women in windows, the sex shops… and more than once I've had requests for the Casa Rosso live sex show. Or, as I like to call it, Bad Porn Live!

Are you someone who is sensitive about explicit sexuality? Amsterdam's live sex shows will desensitize the entire process for you, reducing it to a joyless and purely biological function. Every night at 8 P.M., 10 P.M. and 11:30 P.M.. The acts in the revue shows rotate, much like the bed on the stage. Watching a live sex show, I'm always filled with questions: Was this invented by someone who started in porn but loved theater? Or was it someone from the theater, who really loved porn? Either way, they do put on a show. The partners are introduced rather like figure skaters: "Let's hear it for Tony & Sabrina!" Like figure skaters, they have their chosen music – and act out a number of poses involving legs in the air. And like a *pas de deux* in ballet, it is carefully choreographed. But unlike ballet, these guys go all the way.

The most interesting thing I ever witnessed at the live sex show was the moment the performers got an audience volunteer they weren't expecting. We were there at the show with a group, mostly Americans and some internationals. In the show, there's a joke when one of the couples stops in the middle of sex and asks for a volunteer. Nervous laughter usually follows. But that night, one of the women from our group stood up and said, "Pick me!" And sure enough, she got up onstage, got down on her knees and started going to work. I couldn't tell who was more mortified; the performers onstage or the group of Americans who – as it turned out – would never talk to her again.

By now, I've come up with a solution for my out-of-town guests: the sauna. The Dutch co-ed, naked sauna. It satisfies the need for viewing naked people, and it's good for your skin. It's Dutch Culture Shock Therapy in a nutshell. In fact, the first person who took me to the Dutch sauna was my Dutch boss. And she was very up front about it. She stripped off her clothes, looked us in the eyes and said, "These are my tits. Yes, they're real. And now let's all relax."

I still remember my when my brother visited, and I told him we were going to the Dutch sauna. He said, "Oops, I didn't bring my swimsuit." Because in the US, every day is 'Swimsuit day.' (Back when this story occurred – and Oibibio still existed – there was no 'Swimsuit day.') I told my brother, "No problem. All you need is a towel." But then we went in the locker room, and he panicked: "There are women in here!" I told him, "That's the deal. You get undressed, they get undressed." And then he started enjoying himself. "I'm going to see real naked ladies!"

But quickly there were so many naked females it was overwhelming. So many styles of pubic hair: The triangle, the stripe. The angry spider. Quickly he realized it's not just 'naked ladies.' It's all kinds of naked people. Men, women. Young, old. Skinny, fat. Tattoos, appendectomy scars. And how often do you get to see Grandma naked? It's the real deal.

The sex industry is good business for the Netherlands. They even have trade shows. And sometimes I get to perform for them. In fact, there was one time Boom Chicago was hired for an event called Europerve. The organizers went all-in and had the actors fitted for tailor-made outfits of latex, leather & PVC – even our technician! Unfortunately, I missed the early part of the show, because I had to perform in the home theater that night. But my colleague Lesley Bevan told me what I missed:

"We'd all had appointments at some sex shop to be outfitted in sassy rubber duds. There was a generous amount of talcum powder required to wriggle into them. ... There we were, in a room full of angry looking rubber clad people shifting their weight from side to side, staring at us, and for the most part, silent. (In defense of the guy down front, it's hard to yell out a suggestion with a ball gag in your mouth.)"

I was given a ticket if I wanted to come later, just to see my colleagues in their gear. I had to go! But it was a theme party, and I needed a costume. Specifically, I needed to invent a costume. So – like Cinderella going to the ball – I found my fairy godmother in the form of Frank the house manager. Frank was an artist. Using the theme 'perve,' he looked around the theater for inspiration. Instead of a pumpkin, he found a plastic cactus being used for decor. It helped that his surname was Plant. The plastic cactus was the size of a squat basketball.

Frank took the round, plastic cactus and said, "This is your costume." He cut out a hole for my face, and he placed the cactus ball over my head. He took the cut-out remainder and made it into a codpiece, which I strapped on to my loins. The finishing piece was nothing but some sandals and a cape. I arrived at the event and announced: "I AM CACTUS MAN!" The door man said, "That's the freakiest thing I've seen all night." I was the belle of the Europerve ball. That's Culture Shock Therapy.

CHAPTER 9

DUTCH BIKES
Instant Assimilation

"Then, from behind, a bicycle slammed into me... I turned and saw a young, brunette cyclist in a short skirt. She looked awfully cute. She also looked mighty pissed – at me. She scowled, then muttered '*Klootzak!*' and sped off."

– Pete Jordan, author *De Fietsrepubliek*

I bike. Even in Chicago I used to bike. If ever you've seen the one madman, biking in the middle of a snowstorm, it may have been me. When I came to the Netherlands and saw the standard means of transport was a bike, a part of me felt like I was home.

Going from pedestrian to bicyclist is the most fundamental form of Dutch assimilation. When you first arrive here as a pedestrian, then *yes* you're right: "Dutch people bike like crazy, and I almost got hit by a bike five times, and it's scary." Poor you! But then as soon as you get your own bike, it's immediately: "Stupid tourists! It's called a bike path! Thank goodness I was never that stupid."

Bike lanes are nice, but bike *paths* are sublime. Many cities are now creating bike lanes on their streets. But then you're still in traffic. And you still share your lane with the worst enemy of all: the parked car opening its door. That was the standard when I got here in the '90s. (I still have nightmares about those car doors.) Since then, the Dutch have been constructing more bike *paths* – between the parked cars and the sidewalk. Now, the worst problem is plowing into the occasional pedestrian. But remember, that just makes you more Dutch.

Back in the '90s, my first bike was a 'junkie bike,' freshly curated and stolen by Amsterdam's plentiful selection of junkies. At one point, everyone I knew had a junkie bike. My boss even had one, covered in red and yellow tape. Decorative! That's how I learned a valuable lesson about Amsterdam biking etiquette. My colleague had borrowed the fancy, taped-up bike from our boss. Together, we were riding in the bike lane. But at one point, two pedestrians started shouting at us in Dutch. From the sidewalk. We weren't sure what we'd done wrong, but one of these guys lunged through the parked cars and started grabbing at the bike. It soon became apparent that this pedestrian was – in fact – the one who'd meticulously applied the red and yellow tape, since it was his bike. And he had every reason to believe we ourselves had stolen it. My colleague was trying to explain: "No, I didn't steal the bike! I'm just borrowing the bike. From the guy who paid the junkie who stole your bike…" And after hearing himself, my colleague immediately gave the bike back. We walked back home.

Now we had to explain to our boss what had happened to his bike. He just laughed, "Easy come, easy go. Sorry to put you in that situation." I like to think I've paid for my junkie bike sins, in that I've had so many of my own bikes stolen over the years. Although I guess I can't really call it stealing when I leave my keys in the lock, like an idiot.

BIKE ETIQUETTE

If you spend more time living in the Netherlands, you may want to learn the official rules of the road. You will then know more than many Dutch people do. I was once doing a gig for a corporate event, leading a walking tour through Amsterdam city center. I had Europeans, Americans, Australians. And I was careful to cross the streets at the zebra crossing for pedestrians. Surely that would be safe…?

But then there I was with my group halfway across the Rokin, when I heard the angry bike bell of an older Dutchman coming at me at full speed. All I could do was swat at him with my clipboard as he whipped by me. And then – once I got everyone safely across the bike path – my group was still looking at me with fear. I realized the Dutchman on his bike had turned around to come back and yell at me. He was swearing at me: "You don't have to hit me, *hè*? I am going my own gang! *Je wil met me vechten, hè*? You want to fight?"

My adrenaline surging, I explained: "I just took the Dutch driving exam, and it's very clear: all wheeled traffic must stop when pedestrians are present in a crosswalk, including bikes." I don't know why I thought that would work. Somehow I guess I expected that he would say, "Gosh. You're right. I'm sorry!" But instead we all got to learn the word *Mesjokke!* as he spat at me and took off. I explained to my guests: "*Mesjokke* means crazy person." And we pretended he was talking about himself.

I love it that the Dutch family car is often a bike. There can be child seats on the back of the bike and a baby seat on the front handlebars. Do you need helmets? No. In America, you would be arrested as an unfit parent for biking like this. But here: *Doe normaal*! In fact, sometimes the baby seat on the front handlebars will feature the added protection of a windscreen. "Because wind in the face is dangerous!" But being hit by a truck? Don't worry about it. Dutch police won't stop you for having an un-helmeted baby strapped to the front of your bike, like a human shield. In fact, Dutch police won't stop you if there is one kid on the front handlebars, one on the crossbar, two on the back rack, and another one standing on top of those two for a playdate. In Nederland, that's called 'Wednesday.'

As Nederland is a country of bikes, it makes sense the Dutch have hosted the opening of the Tour de France. In fact, I don't know why there's no Tour de Nederland – a Dutch version of the Tour de France. No racing bikes, no helmets. Just the typical Dutch mama trying to get three kids to school, balanced on one bike, through the cold and the wind and the rain that somehow comes at you horizontally. As far as I know, there are no plans for a 'Tour de Nederland.' But if there's any country that would make `Biking to School' into a national championship, it would be Nederland.

There was one bike trick I saw in the street in front of my house, and I still can't believe it. There was a dad riding the bike, a toddler on the front handlebars, and on the back rack was the mom, holding a little baby. The baby couldn't have been more than six months old. Then the mama took her hand off the papa, so she was just balancing on her butt. I thought, "This is like watching Cirque du Soleil." Why did she remove her hand from the Papa? So that she could reach over, pull up her shirt and start breast-feeding.

Yes. That is how the Dutch roll. Were they stopped by the police? No. But if they'd been riding at night without a light? That's a fine of € 50.

CHAPTER 10
DUTCH LANGUAGE
Dunglish

"Would it be easier if we just do this in English?"

– 90% of Dutch people

Ik praat wel nederlands, hoor. But I don't like to speak Dutch. It makes my mouth feel sad.

Esthetically, the Dutch language makes an awful first impression. It's that guttural *G* sound. Europe has a lovely selection of 'Romance Languages,' which does not include *Nederlands*. But maybe it should. Because – with the guttural *G* – you're exchanging bodily fluids with your speaking partner – romantic!

Actually, I assume the *G* sound was first developed as a biological defense mechanism. And the further north you go, the harder is the *G*. When Amsterdammers say, "Good morning" it comes out "ggggoeie morggggen," making them sound like angry choking victims. I love Dutch people, and I love Dutch culture ...but Nederland, you deserve a better language.

My wife says I have a love / hate relationship with the Dutch language. I think that's not fair. I'd call it hate / hate. I don't love the Dutch language, but in the spirit of the Netherlands, I tolerate it. What is not tolerated is practicing your bad Dutch on 90% of Dutch people. I fully recognize and respect the right of Dutch people to demand that I learn the lan-

guage. But in practice, as soon as I speak Dutch, they quickly beg me to stop. Or – when I'm in the train and offering to sit facing backwards – I make one small verbal mistake, and everyone laughs at me for some reason.

It can be hard to practice Dutch with Dutch people. When you speak Dutch poorly, that's when the famous tolerance ends. Then it's: "Would it be easier if we just do this in English?" It even happens in my home. We're raising our kids to be bilingual. Mama speaks her native language with the kids, and Papa speaks his language. So when I try practicing my Dutch at home, it's my kids who cover their ears and say, "Papa, stop!" I had to get a dog. With the dog I can speak Dutch.

By this point, my command of the Dutch language is 'best good' (which is Dutch for 'neither best, nor good'). The Dutch language I speak could best be called Dunglish. Otherwise known as 'Google Translate Nederlands.' By that I mean: "ALL words the required ARE in sentence located. BUT in the order correct NOT to be seem." When I speak Dutch, so I'm told, I *sound* authentic enough that many Dutch people assume I'm a native speaker, who may have a head injury. I'll start out making sense. I'll try to say: "I went to university. I'm reasonably intelligent." But what comes out in Dutch is: "I've been to the universe. I am intelligence." And they look at me weird.

Just as I speak 'Google Translate Dutch,' there are some Dutch people who speak Google Translate English. And there are plenty of wonderful books about that. You've probably heard the story of the Dutchman who tells the Brit, "I like to fok horses." I've even heard a story about a Dutchman who walked into a British furniture store and asked for a baby bed, using the Dutch word *ledikant*. To the Brits, the man was asking for a 'ladyc_nt.' And they called the police.

I once had to interview Amsterdam Mayor Eberhard van der Laan onstage. It was an English-language event, but he insisted on speaking Dutch. Offstage he told me, "My English is okay, but I had a speech coach who told me, 'There's nothing more dangerous than Dutch people who think they can speak English *fluid*.'"

The previous mayor was more ambitious. Mayor Job Cohen once hosted an international event, and he spoke English. He came out onstage, and instead of saying, "Good evening, good evening," he said, "Good night, good night." He got a huge laugh. And he smiled, as if to say, "Yes, I know I'm funny." But we were in the audience thinking, "that was the shortest speech ever..."

And then there's Prime Minister Mark Rutte. He is a role model for all of us Dunglish speakers. Rutte once said, according to *De Volkskrant*: "I worked ten years for Unilever, largely in English. If you're constantly trying to translate your thoughts, it often slows down your thinking." Hence Rutte's tendency to mix and match languages. Rutte once referred to a minister in his Cabinet as a member of his '*administratie*.' In America, the Cabinet is 'The Administration.' But in the Netherlands, *administratie* means bookkeepers – aka 'bean counters.' This is a great example of a *gaffe,* aka 'when a politician accidentally tells the truth.'

And so Dunglish lives on. Asked to eradicate Dunglish from his vocabulary, Rutte once replied, "*Ik doe mijn best*... but it's a tall order."

CHAPTER 11

DUTCH MEETINGS Are from Mars

"For most cultures, a decision is the end of the discussion. For the Dutch it's just the beginning."

– V. Bekker, NiNsee Institute

Dutch office culture is, to me, based on paradox. How can a meeting start out so productive, but then end so differently?

I've had the pleasure of attending meetings in a few different cultures. As an amateur cultural anthropologist, I've noticed that business meetings are a bit like sex: sometimes you have to seduce your negotiating partner. In that sense, Dutch meetings are from Mars; Belgian meetings are from Venus.

In Belgium – even Flanders – I've found that the culture is more inspired by the French. Belgian meetings are more like foreplay for women:

Yes, your meeting starts with coffee, but it's nice coffee. Espresso coffee. You drink your coffee at a café table, where you can watch your coffee being made, just for you. A conference room? *Non!* No one's thinking about that right now. Tell me, what would you like with your coffee? Perhaps a cookie? Not just any cookie, but a nice cookie. Nothing you have to unwrap – these were made fresh, just for you. And you look like you might enjoy some of our fine chocolate as well. Perhaps there's a menu for the fine selection of fine chocolates to go with your fine coffee, just for you. Take your time, what's the rush? How was your journey? How are you feeling? What's on your mind? Business, you say? *Oui, oui!* Let me take you to my conference room...

Dutch meetings are like foreplay for men: "Here's some coffee. Let's get to business! Business! Business! (cheese sandwich) Business! Ahh... That was good business. Want a cigarette? The smoking area is outside. *Doei!*"

In the Netherlands, it's Business First – *Gezelligheid* Second. Sometimes so much gets done, so quickly, they celebrate by scheduling meetings just for the sake of revisiting everything that got done.

NON-HIERARCHICAL

I once saw a corporate speaker who had done a survey of Dutch companies, asking: "What's the most important factor for your Job Satisfaction?" He'd offered choices such as Salary, Diversity, Cafeteria Quality... But the most important factor for Dutch workers was Autonomy. Self-determination. "Yes, I'll help you realize your idea. But how we get there is MY idea." Apparently, this trend goes all the way back to the revolt against the Spanish occupation: Dutch folks don't like people telling them what to do. Most countries are rather hierarchical: the boss says it and you do it. Not the Dutch! The Dutch are so flat that even a town called '7 Mountains' is actually under sea level.

QUESTION EVERYTHING

In a way, being non-hierarchical promotes equality. In decision-making, there's an emphasis on consensus. In the Netherlands, there will be no agreement on an idea, then they'll debate the idea until they unanimously agree, then the next day they'll change their minds and do something completely different. Yes, everyone should agree on everything. Yet – far from being agreeable – many Dutch meetings I've attended feature the most negative, contrary, cynical conversations I've ever had. American meetings will sometimes end with, "Let's agree to disagree." Dutch meetings are more like, "Let's disagree to agree."

There's a phrase I've heard to describe Dutch meetings: "*Iedereen moet z'n plasje erover doen.*" Or: "Everyone gets a chance to piss on your idea." And if an idea can stand up to that treatment, then it deserves to be taken seriously. However, this treatment can come as a shock for international colleagues. It's one thing for Brussels to have *Manneke Pis,* peeing statue; it's another thing to act it out at every meeting.

SECOND-GUESS EVERYTHING

The downside of the non-hierarchical Dutch management style is that hard decisions can be hard to come by. Put another way, Dutch folks change their minds so much it's a miracle anything gets done.

I've been to Dutch meetings where everyone agrees on a proposal so quickly it makes them uncomfortable. You could tell the managers are feeling: "This can't be right!" Then, sure enough, someone says, "*Ja, maar…*" Or: "Yes, but…" It's like every Dutch manager grows up with an inner insurance salesman – a little built-in Actuary to calculate every possible risk. Here's a meeting I've attended more than once:

"We'd like to hire this comedian for our event! He can make all the jokes we can't say in front of the boss."

"Yes, but what if he's not funny?"

"Yes, but what if our audience has no sense of humor?"

"Yes, but what if there's someone in the audience who's having an affair with someone else in the audience and he makes a joke about inter-office affairs and they are offended?" (actual quote)

Since they're so non-hierarchical, every Dutch person at a Dutch meeting gets to debate every decision. Dutch emails are like: "I know what we agreed at the meeting, but I have had some different thoughts about the meeting since the meeting, so I think we should have another meeting to make sure everyone still agrees with the meeting, and then a follow-up meeting to change what we agreed at the meeting, and then another meeting to review the meeting about the meeting." And the email is written by the intern who's only been working there two weeks.

SOME CASE STUDIES

Granted I'm just a comedian, but I do get some lovely, candid snapshots of corporate life in the Netherlands – by performing at the bizarrely revealing rituals known as 'Dutch corporate events.' Let me take you on a mini tour.

THE NON-HIERARCHICAL

I was helping make a video for a Dutch innovation: ULT Freezers that are water-cooled, instead of air-cooled. Since freezers produce heat, these Dutch engineers thought, "Why not remove the heat with water? Then, effectively, the freezer doubles as a water heater." This simple design change would cut costs and help the environment. The result? "No thanks!" Why? Because the Dutch engineers were working for a Japanese company. According to the Dutch team, there the ideas are supposed to go Top-Down, not Bottom-Up. Last I heard they were taking the idea to Philips. While many cultures have 'top-down management,' the Dutch way can be more innovative.

THE QUESTION EVERYTHING

I was once hired to perform some tailored standup for a product launch. At least that's what I'd thought, because that's what the boss told me. But then the boss invited me to a conference call to explain the idea to her colleagues. And I listened as they all took turns second-guessing her plan, until it was time to go, and – instead of being hired – I was 'Maybe Hired.'

I once heard a saying: "A camel is a horse, designed by a committee." That's what they were attempting in the conference call. The boss wanted tailored stand-up. But her colleague wanted a live role-play. I lost the job. I found out later that the client really wanted neither stand-up nor role play, but an animated video. I guess I'm just glad I could help them figure out what they didn't want.

THE SECOND-GUESS EVERYTHING

I was hired with Boom Chicago to do a Christmas show for a major fashion label. Apparently, there were rumors that the Dutch office might be closing, and everyone's jobs were at risk. Luckily, the rumors were not true! At the show, the boss would give the good news, and then introduce us to help celebrate. One day later, the organizing committee had changed their minds: Since we were Americans, the boss would introduce us as upper management from the New York office. Then we'd address the bad rumors, and the boss would reveal it's a joke and give the good news. Weird, but okay!

Then – on the day of the show – the idea had changed again. The boss did introduce us as upper management from New York. But then he lied to his entire staff and said, "You're all being laid off." Next, he laughed and left the stage. We had to cut in and say, "It's a joke! We're hired comedians." And then we had to do a comedy show. Dear reader, if you can think of a worse way to start a comedy show, please insert that image here. (For example, he could have yelled, "Fire!" Or he could have actually lit the theater on fire.) The result? The audience hated us. But the boss seemed genuinely happy.

THE SOMEWHAT HIERARCHICAL

I once hosted an event with the Dutch King in attendance. Since Dutch society is so non-hierarchical, you'd expect Dutch business leaders to be relaxed about it. You'd be wrong. There were so many pre-meetings and protocols! Before the King entered the room, I had to read off a whole list in front of the audience: When to stand, when not to stand; What to say, what not to say. After going through the list with the audience, I remarked, "Wow, this guy is high-maintenance." And the King was there in the wings, and the King laughed! I did the show, and then I had the line, "Well, the King has a busy schedule, so let us all rise as he leaves the theater."

Willem-Alexander, sitting in the front row, was apparently taken by surprise. He looked around, as if to say, "I have to leave now? I just got here." But then his entourage arose and escorted him away. Part of me wonders if the King would have preferred to dispense with the formalities and just *doe maar gewoon*. But not as long as everyone around him is so formal. I was left thinking, "Hey, let's not bow down too low – don't forget we're the ones paying his salary."

CHAPTER 12

DUTCH HOUSING and Full-Frontal Nudity

'Ieder huisje heeft zijn kruisje'

– Dutch expression

I've lived in ten places since I arrived in the Netherlands. Each one taught me a lesson about being Dutch.

HOUSE 1 DUTCH MEN ARE *WATJES*

The first place I ever lived in the Netherlands was a brand-new building. We were the first ones to live there. It felt like Amsterdam was saying, "Welcome! We built this place just for you!" Boom Chicago had arranged the place for a group of us. There were three spacious bedrooms, a spacious kitchen, and teeny, tiny stairs. Apparently, the place was meant for a newlywed couple, but something had gone wrong with the timing, and that's why they needed renters. It was explained to us that – though the place was fully furnished – some of the furnishings hadn't yet been unwrapped. Specifically, we noticed that the dinner plates were in gift wrap saying, 'Congratulations to the happy couple!' We felt bad as we sat opening someone else's gifts, but we couldn't wait to hear the story behind the place.

At one point, we had to deliver our rent to the owner – the former bride-to-be. She was a tall, blond doctor. Apparently, the would-be groom was a doctor, too. Cautiously, we asked... "What the hell happened?" She told us: her parents had bought the house for the happy couple, with not just a master bedroom – but two separate bedrooms for the kids they'd be having. That's when her fiancé had had a 'fear of commitment' and broken up with her. And then we got a long and spirited rant, introducing us to her theory that – as Dutch women had become liberated – Dutch men had become 'cotton ball' *watjes*.

A few years later, I was subletting a place with a friend of mine. We were subletting from a woman who'd moved in with her boyfriend. It was a nice place, fully furnished, and it was all going well... until one night there was the woman, crying in our living room. "We broke up," she explained. "He threw me out!" We tried to console her, "Aww... there, there." And around midnight, still sniffling, she looked up at us and said, "So – where are you guys going to stay tonight?" Dutch relationships. Sometimes they giveth. Sometimes they taketh away.

HOUSE 2 THE POOP PEDESTAL

In the second place Boom Chicago arranged, there was an even bigger group of us. This place was right behind the Victorieplein in the Rivierenbuurt district. We'd heard Rivierenbuurt was a pretty quiet neighborhood, and this spot was perhaps the quietest. The five of us had the whole house to ourselves. The stairs were even narrower and steeper. My room, in fact, was accessed by a plain-old ladder. Why not just be honest and make them all ladders?

The south-facing balconies looked out to a lush, green courtyard, and as soon as we got into the house, we flung open the doors and cranked up some tunes – Beastie Boys, I believe. It was perhaps 15 seconds before the angry banging began. It was not the last time the neighbors would protest at us Loud Americans.

Our second place was the first time I'd encountered a phenomenon I'd never heard of before: the Rent Police. One day there was a knock on the door. My roommate opened it and announced the police wanted to come in. I assumed it was due to the neighbors complaining about the noise. But no, said the Rent Police, they wanted to check the details of our rental agreement. That sounded even worse! They asked how many of us were living in the place, how many were allowed to live there, and how much we were each paying. I said I'd feel more comfortable answering these questions if our bosses were present, as they were the ones who'd arranged the rental. The Rent Police then explained the reason they were there: to protect us from our bosses. That's what the Rent

Police are all about: not kicking people out, but making sure people are not being made to pay too much. What a concept. I felt more at home than ever.

Our second place was famous. Anne Frank had once lived on our street. The Merwedeplein was where the Frank family lived before they went into hiding. As a sort of testament to her memory, there was an old synagogue around the corner, which was of course abandoned. At first, we thought of it as a chilling reminder what had happened to the Jewish population of Amsterdam. But after a while, we realized that there are still plenty of Jews in Rivierenbuurt. It's just that – like most secular Dutch folks – they'd rather be dead than seen in a place of worship. I believe the former synagogue is now an auction house. Literally, there are moneylenders in the temple.

And our second place was the first time I had to live with The Shelf. Dutch culture is well known for treating sex as a natural part of life. Less well-known is that there's a similar attitude toward the toilet.

I come from a country where going to the toilet is known as 'going to the bathroom.' The Dutch have no such linguistic confusion. In fact – in our house – the designers had gone to the trouble of separating out the bath and putting the toilet in its own, separate room. This was so we could learn to say, "I'm going to the toilet" – and so that the process of pooping could be made unavoidably, distractingly pungent. Our toilet chamber was designed to be as tiny as possible. Frequently, my knees would knock the birthday calendar from the door. The exhaust fan was a lovely antique, possibly on the world heritage list, since it was clearly impossible to update or renovate it in any way. It was a callback to an earlier time, when exhaust fans were scheduled to revolve based on the lunar calendar. Once a month, you might hear a small *Erp*.

And then, of course, there was the famous Dutch inspection shelf. As I've read, it was designed as a shelf to inspect one's poop – for making sure one's poop is 'on the level.' When Freud invented the term anal-retentive, it is well possible he was referring to a Dutch patient. Whereas the rest of the world finds such a practice scatological and repulsive, the Dutch seem keen to pride themselves on what they've accomplished.

Granted, the inspection shelf is not as common, these days. But Dutch manufacturers still do make the things. Recently, I went on a trip to a home improvement center, and there they were on display. I had to check if maybe they were old models that someone was trying to get rid of. But no, they were new. Clearly there's still a demand for the Dutch poop pedestal. There was even a toilet design named Carice. You may know Carice van Houten for her role as Lady Melisandre on *Game of Thrones*. Were the designers going for a pun on the word *Thrones*? Possibly. But I could only think of her *Game of Thrones* catchphrase, as it applies to the inspection shelf: "The night is dark and full of terrors."

In our current house we still have a toilet with an inspection shelf. Our house is like many old, Dutch houses built on sand: it leans over to one side. Thus, our toilet 'shelf' has become a toilet 'slope,' angled backward. Or – if you will – it's a like toilet 'stunt ramp.' Every time we flush, it's an adventure: will our brown heroes make it over the edge into freedom?

Americans have been accused of being loud and arrogant, as summed up in the phrase 'They think their shit don't stink.' But to our defense – at least it's submerged in water.

HOUSE 3 GOLDEN AGE HOUSING

My third apartment in Amsterdam was a short-stay. For a few weeks, I lived right in Amsterdam center – on the Nieuwendijk, by the Singel. It was a 17th-century building, straight from the Golden Age. And it hadn't been properly fixed up since then. Trying to feel at home in that tiny space was like trying to atone for some previous sins. Specifically, the sins of being too loud the year before. That apartment was the noisiest place I've ever experienced. For example, I had no problem hearing everyone in the building while they were having sex. I could even tell which neighbors enjoyed spanking. Now, I'll never think of the Golden Age the same way.

On Queen's Day (now King's Day), it was so loud outside the walls were vibrating. Not in a good way. I'd woken up hung over from the Queen's Night party the night before, and I'd soon realized I was in the epicenter of Ground Zero of the noise quake – right in between a stack of speakers blaring techno beats and a concert stage they'd set up for Dutch *schlager* music. It was not a good match. For anyone who's ever considered being hung over and then remixing the awful, saccharine Dutch *smartlappen* with poorly syncopated house beats, I don't recommend it. Luckily, it was Queen's Day, so I left the house and continued drinking. I moved out of there the next day.

HOUSE 4 THE STADSREGISTER

Next came my experience 'outside the ring,' literally looking out onto the ring road of Amsterdam. If you've ever been on the highway, looked out at the charmless '70s high-rise tower blocks and wondered, "Who lives there?" That was me.

This time my roommate and I were subletting from a pair of students on one condition: we had to pretend we were houseguests. The students were what I would call rich-kid *kakkers*. And they were very clear: "Whatever happens, do NOT tell anyone we're taking our housing subsidy and using it to live in Ibiza." In retrospect – when the city required me to give a fixed address to the Stadsregister – I probably shouldn't have given their address. Because those guys subsequently got in a lot of trouble. But don't worry: I'm sure they're now very successful in Dutch banking. Or perhaps the Dutch Building Sector.

At the time, I didn't realize the importance of the Dutch Stadsregister, where the civil servants approach their jobs with a unique level of scrutiny. There is a chronic shortage of Dutch housing, partly because

Dutch people treat housing like they treat their bikes: they move in with each other and get new ones, without getting rid of the old ones first. As a result, the Stadsregister demands many forms of documentation. The sheer amount of documentation is designed to convince you to move somewhere else. You will need passport, birth certificate, signatures from witnesses, and perhaps even an apostille.

The term apostille comes from the riddle 'Which follower of Jesus was actually French?' Only if you answer correctly, may you reside in the Netherlands. Note: being registered at the Stadsregister is not the same as having a *verblijfsvergunning* (residence permit). In other words, you may have permission to live here, but you do not have permission to stay.

HOUSE 5 THE HOUSEBOAT

For a week I lived on a houseboat in the Amstel, right across from *De IJsbreker*. I'd always thought of 'Ice breaker' in terms of 'conversation starter.' But since it was November when I moved in and the river was almost freezing, I soon thought of *De IJsbreker* in terms of the ship that plows a path through the ice. There were houseboats next to us, which were the more modern structures, built on floating concrete foundations. But our houseboat was a real boat, docked to the riverbank and displacing water. I'd enter through the wheelhouse and the kitchen. Then I'd climb down the stairs to the ship's hold, which was the main floor. I remember looking out the porthole windows and seeing the water at eye level. It seemed surreal to me. For one thing, the whole city was under sea level. To park your home under river level just seemed like tempting fate. It was actually surprisingly spacious and comfortable, but I had to move out after a week.

HOUSE 6 THE MISSING FLOOR

In 1997, I came across the nastiest apartment I'd ever seen. It was in Amsterdam Oost on a street called Vrolikstraat, or 'Cheerful Street.' If anyone had ever been cheerful there, it would have been a long time ago. The place was in a row of 19th-century working class houses, some of which were being gutted and fixed up. Not ours! The front door opened, and the stairs smelled like a wet cave. The crooked staircase led us up to a completely empty apartment – except for the balcony, which was completely full – full – of pigeon droppings. Years of pigeon poop. Pigeon poop atop stacks and stacks of pigeon poop. Our jaws dropped. There was a net to keep the pigeons out, but someone had somehow ripped a huge hole in it. Obviously, that someone was the pierced and unwashed woman showing us the place, who explained, "Pigeons need a place to live too." Taking note of our still-dropped jaws, she casually suggested, "You can clean it if you want."

Somehow, my roommate convinced me to take the place with the rationale "We just won't go on the balcony." And "Anyway, the floors are beautiful." And he was right. The solid oak planks were lovely. And they were gone. When we moved in they were just ... gone. That was my introduction to the Dutch version of *unfurnished*. They even take the floorboards. All they'd left was just particleboard laid over the crossbeams. "Oh yeah, didn't we tell you? We took the floors with us." No, they didn't tell us. But we figured it out. And we got out as soon as possible.

HOUSE 7 SQUATTING YOUR OWN HOME

From the east side, I moved to the northwest in the charming neighborhood called Bos en Lommer. Here we found ourselves renting from a circus duo, named Vincent & Marli. It was a nice, big place ... but there was a catch. The circus wasn't doing so well, so they'd moved into the tiny storage space upstairs, to live rent-free. The deal was: we had the place to ourselves – unless they needed to use the toilet. Or unless they needed to use the kitchen. Or unless they needed to rehearse their act in the spacious living room. To be fair, they were on the road a lot, so it was a pretty good deal for us. And when they'd rehearse, it was amazing. He was a huge dude with a Las Vegas hairdo, and she was a tiny Eastern European girl with a lot of makeup. We'd wake up, hung over, on Saturday mornings, and he'd be throwing her all over the place. We loved it.

HOUSE 8 HOUSE OF BASS

Vincent & Marli the circus couple started getting paid more, so they moved back downstairs and kicked us out. That was around the time I fell in love with a Dutch woman – who owned her own apartment. I moved in almost immediately. The apartment was also in Bos en Lommer, on the 3rd floor, above a tram stop. Our downstairs neighbors were from Aruba, from a family that seemed to keep growing. The father was a brown, pudgy man with wild hair and a penchant for loud Latin music. Music with a lot of bass. He wasn't the only one in the family with this condition. One day their family had grown into the storage space above us with a teenage boy who liked deep house music – with a lot of bass. We'd just had our first child, and our bedroom was being bombarded from above and from below. We'd be polite and knock on the door below. The father would always accommodate by turning the music down – not realizing that the bass was still as prominent as ever. This process repeated itself constantly.

One Saturday afternoon, we'd finally gotten our six-month-old to lie down for a nap, when the bass kicked off again from below. Our daughter woke up right away. This time we thought we'd do something different. We'd all three of us go downstairs to knock on the door. So we did. When our neighbor whipped open the door and said, "YES?" ...he was stark naked. With a condom in his hand.

But, apparently, he hadn't expected to see me AND my wife. And he certainly didn't expect a six-month-old girl. "OK, I'll turn it down," he said. "NO," my wife insisted. "Leave it. Leave it JUST like it is and come with me." The naked neighbor grabbed a robe and trudged upstairs with us. And we ushered him into our bedroom, being bombarded by sound waves. It was at that moment that he got it. Months' worth of sympathy and shame flooded his eyes, as he said, "*Nou – da's wel gehorig.*" ("Wow, that's pretty loud.") He looked at us with a quizzical expression that seemed to say, "How did you survive?" We looked back at him, equally quizzically – saying, "We don't know." And then he went back to his chores.

HOUSE 9 BUILD A WALL, CHARGE SOME RENT

My wife and I found the house of our dreams, but – before we could move in – we'd need to do some renovating. My wife's father said we could stay with him for six months – if he could do some renovating too. Previously, he had expanded his flat by buying the floor upstairs. Now, he just needed to wall off half of his upstairs area, which was just big enough for a tiny apartment for us. I've seen it happen more often in the Netherlands: when times are tough, build a wall and charge rent.

But now the question was: Would I be willing to move in with my wife's family? It all seemed so 'Old Europe.' On the plus side, I was looking at my father in-law and thinking 'live-in babysitter.' He was looking at me and thinking 'compulsive stoop-cleaner.' My father in-law also recommended the contractors he'd used to build his wall. Not Dutch contractors, they were too expensive! "The cheaper Eastern European workers are just as good." I remember their van had a logo featuring the word *Bouwers* (builders) with a picture of a man busy doing demolition. Not an auspicious beginning.

HOUSE 10 *GOEDKOOP IS DUURKOOP*

We finally moved into our new home in June 2003. That was when we learned the Dutch lesson called *Goedkoop is duurkoop:* Being cheap can be expensive. The shower on the upper floor wasn't properly sealed, and we'd later have to pay for years of hidden water damage. The bathroom tiles had been installed backwards, with the shiny bits sticking to the wall. And when it was time to move in, the 'builders' weren't finished yet. For one thing, there were big nails sticking out of the fence where our kids would play. "No problem, we fix!" said the Russian builders.

The Russians just needed to go out for some supplies. They announced that they needed to drive over to the hardware store, and they'd be right back. They were not right back. After a few hours, they showed up, battered and traumatized. There had been a car accident. The accident had involved a tram. In his heavy Russian accent, our man explained exactly what had happened: "The tram – it came out of nowhere!"

Despite the rails in the middle of the street – normally a pretty clear indicator of where the tram might be coming from – the Russians had been foiled! The only question on my mind was: at what point had they started drinking? Perhaps they'd started drinking after the accident to calm their nerves. Or perhaps they'd been drinking before that. Either way, the smell of vodka was wafting off of them with every failed attempt to explain. Soon, they'd conjured up an image of the tram having willed itself off its rails in a long-contemplated act of miraculous liberation. Needless to say, no work got done that day. But I couldn't help sympathizing with the Russians. After having dealt with magically gift-wrapped dish sets, disappearing floorboards and living room circus acts – who's to say that there are no Flying Trams in Amsterdam?

CHAPTER 13

THE GREAT ZWARTE PIET DEBATE

6 to 8 Soot-Faced Men

"The six to eight Black men were characterized as personal slaves until... the political climate changed, and it was decided that instead of being slaves they were just good friends."

– David Sedaris, 2004

Dutch culture is famous for its pragmatic solutions to thorny social problems. ... And then there's *Zwarte Piet.* Or 'Black Pete.' While much of Dutch society is trying – and succeeding – to be color-blind, Black Pete occupies a 'Color Blind Spot.' Here is an overview.

THE GASLIGHTING CEREMONY

The Dutch Santa Claus is called *Sinterklaas,* and every November he arrives on his magical steamboat from Spain. And just as Santa Claus has his magical selves, Sinterklaas has – what appears to be – an army of Black slaves. What comes next is a parade – and a textbook example of *gaslighting.* "They're not slaves," Dutch people will insist, pointing to the tall white man on his big white horse, surrounded by Black people doing all the work. "They're just his *negers.*" The word *neger* is not offensive, because it simply means 'Black person.' And besides, "They're not really Black people! They're just white people in blackface."

I remember a science fiction film, where there are hideous aliens who emit a substance that makes humans think they're adorable. Sinterklaas seems to emit a similar substance that works specifically on Dutch people. Most months of the year, Dutch culture is comparatively inclusive and tolerant. But as soon as Sinterklaas shows up, Dutch folks are slapping on blackface, thinking, "This couldn't possibly be offensive to anyone."

For years, I've been performing shows at Boom Chicago Comedy Theater, making jokes about Zwarte Piet. The most entertaining bit is always after the show, when Dutch people will passionately argue that Zwarte Piet is not really Black: "It's just the soot from the chimney!" Ah yes, the magical soot. It gets all over his face – and not on his clothes. His clothes remain just as shiny and new as in the iconic 1850 children's book *Sinterklaas and His Servant*. And of course, it must be the soot that gives Zwarte Piet his big red lips and hoop earrings and afro…?

I watched my first Sinterklaas parade in 1997, with my Dutch girlfriend. When I said, "That looks like slavery," she told me, "Of course *you* would say that! You're from America, where your country owned slaves! We Dutch never owned slaves. (…We just sold you the slaves.)" In 1998, my girlfriend and I both watched the parade again – this time with Boom Chicago's first African-American comedian Holly Walker. When Holly said, "That looks like slavery," my girlfriend reacted in a unique way: she listened instead of arguing. So I married her.

It's important to note that not all Black people have a problem with Zwarte Piet. I was once dressed as Sinterklaas for a video shoot, and a Black woman came running up to me to ask – unironically – "Can I be your Piet?" But it's also important to note that – for some people – the blackface really is a big problem. Soon after hiring Holly Walker, Boom Chicago added African-American comedians Jordan Peele and then Colton Dunn. Each of them had the same, stunned reaction to Zwarte Piet. And – as more and more Dutch people noticed Black people's reactions – I noticed this amazing transformation. It was rather like Neo waking up from *The Matrix* and pulling out his feeding tube: "Whoa! How could I have not noticed this is totally revolting?" And speaking of revolting, in 2002, Colton and Jordan teamed up with Pep Rosenfeld to make a rap video in which two Black Petes put Sinterklaas in the Naughty Sack and take him back to Spain.

In 2011 – two years before #BlackLivesMatter – another young Black man tried to put Sinterklaas in the Naughty Sack. His name was Quinsy Gario. Trigger warning for Zwarte Piet fans – Quinsy Gario attended a Sinterklaas parade with signs saying 'Zwarte Piet is Racism.' Dutch police responded by tackling him and subjecting him to police brutality. Or – if you still believe Zwarte Piet couldn't possibly be offensive – let's just say the police hoisted him on their shoulders and said, "We respect your opinion."

And let's be super-clear here: most Black people I've talked to do not have a problem with the *existence* of Zwarte Piet, but with the *appearance* of Zwarte Piet. Specifically, they've each had to deal with the unique cultural phenomenon of cute little Dutch kids pointing at them on the street and yelling, "Zwarte Piet!" If you don't believe me, watch Colton or Jordan talking about it on TV. Or watch Amber Ruffin talk about it on *Late Night with Seth Meyers*: "If there was a chimney that applied brown foundation, a perfect afro, hoop earrings and lipstick – I'd have found it already. I'd use it every morning."

THE FALSE POSITIVE

In 2012, I was invited to speak at a cultural event about Zwarte Piet – 'The Great Zwarte Piet Debate!' The event was called '*Zwart van Roet*' (black from soot). And the host was Quinsy Gario, of the 'Zwarte Piet is Racism' protest. Quinsy zeroed in on the crux of the Zwarte Piet issue: The False Positive. For there is one big question, even if you love Zwarte Piet: What should you do, as a person of color, when Dutch people point at you in public and falsely identify you as 'Zwarte Piet?' This is a lesson they do not teach you in Dutch assimilation class.

Right on cue, there were white people at the event saying, "Surely no one points at you and says Zwarte Piet!" And there were Black people saying, "It happens *all the time*."

- An African man: "When Dutch kids point and say 'Zwarte Piet,' I tell them I'm off-duty: No hat, No feather, No Piet."
- An Antillean man: "One kid pointed at me in the café, and I told him 'No presents for you this year!' Then the parents complained, and I was the one who got in trouble."
- A Surinamese man: "I go straight to the parents. I tell them 'This is why you should hire me for your Sinterklaas party. You don't want someone in blackface. You want the real deal. But fair warning: the real black face costs extra.'"

For the win! This man's response was the most Dutch: facing up to a thorny social situation by finding a way to make money from it.

I myself didn't believe little kids would point at Black people and say, "Zwarte Piet" – until I had little kids, and they did it in front of me. That's why Quinsy had invited me to share the story of my False Positive – the time we had 'Zwarte Piet' come to our door.

My Dutch girlfriend became my Dutch wife, and – according to her – we would celebrate Sinterklaas in the 'traditional Dutch way.' That is to say, as simply as possible. We'd get a sack full of presents and we'd give it to the neighbor. The neighbor would wait five minutes and drop the sack at our door. He'd ring the doorbell and run like hell. The kids would then open the door and – even with no one there – they'd scream and cheer and yell, "Thank you!" No costumes, no hired actors. Leave it to the Dutch. It's the most cost-effective special effect ever.

One year, when my daughter was three, we finished dinner early and got ready for presents and Zwarte Piet and gifts. It was almost 6 o'clock, it was already dark, and – before my wife could say, "Zwarte Piet will be here soon," we heard the doorbell ring. My wife looked at me to ask, "Did you go to the neighbor already?" I shook my head no. But my daughter – being three years old – was already at the door. She yelled, "Yay!" and whipped open the front door. And there, standing in the doorway, was a guy with a black face, dark curly hair and a brightly colored red & yellow outfit.

The outfit said 'DHL Post.'

I don't know whose decision it was to send this guy out delivering DHL packages on the 5th of December. I don't know what this guy was thinking taking this shift on the 5th of December. But I do know what my daughter was thinking. Her eyes filled with joy, her lungs filled with air, and my soul filled with dread. I felt like a Secret Service agent, as I lunged myself into the breach. I was looking at my daughter, willing her not to say it, but I wasn't quick enough. She raised her hand and yelled, "Zwarte Piet!"

I was paralyzed, locked in awkward eye contact with the DHL guy. I felt the blood drain from my face, making me somehow even whiter. The American in me was thinking, "No! My daughter is a racist!" But the Dutch part of me was saying, "That's right! It IS Zwarte Piet! Sometimes Papa has to sign Zwarte Piet's Magic Clipboard! And tonight, just to be nice, Papa is going to give Zwarte Piet a tip!" I gave him 5 euros, and I shut the door as quickly as I could. I looked at my wife to ask, "What should I have done?" We agreed it was awkward and we would set our daughter straight. But my wife was mad at me because "Why would you just give away 5 euros?"

THE DISCONNECT

Back at the '*Zwart van Roet*' event, host Quinsy Gario initiated a ritual that would be played out countless times on Dutch talk shows: confronting white people with his perspective on Zwarte Piet – and watching white people have something like a stroke. A stroke is normally a terrible thing, but the Zwarte Piet debate has shown how some white people can willfully shut down selective parts of the brain on command. It's amazing to witness. I was reading an article from a science magazine about people who had temporarily lost access to their brain's right hemisphere. The result was a lack of emotional engagement and an increase in extreme rationalization. This behavior is basically what I witnessed when Quinsy interviewed Jeroen, the director of the Zwarte Piet kids show *Sinterklaas Journaal*.

Jeroen of *Sinterklaas Journaal* started off by explaining that Dutch people do not see Zwarte Piet as Black, insisting: "It's just the soot from the chimney." Next, Jeroen denied that the makeup for Zwarte Piet is called '*Neger Zwart*.' Quinsy called for the technician to do a real-time Google search on the screens onstage, and within five seconds there were several examples of makeup called '*Neger Zwart*.' By the end, Jeroen admitted that – maybe – his depiction of Zwarte Piet could be problematic for 'certain' people. He then complimented Quinsy by saying, "This was an intelligent debate. I must admit, I'd assumed you'd all be just a bunch of '*Bijlmer* types.'"

Since then, the kids' shows have adapted – as they always have. At first, Zwarte Piet would punish kids by putting them in the sack and taking them to Spain. But that had to change, once enough kids realized: "Spain is great! Best vacation ever! How naughty do I have to be to go in the sack with Piet?" Since 2012, it was explained to the kids that the TV Zwarte Piet is *not a Black person*. Next came Zwarte Piet with soot on his face instead of black makeup! They changed the appearance of Zwarte Piet, not the existence of Zwarte Piet. And what do you know – Dutch kids have no problem adapting. But Dutch adults keep having a selective stroke.

BUCK-TOOTH DUTCHIE

In particular, many online comments I've received argue that Soot-faced Piet is not the real Piet. "He should go back to the way he used to look!" And at this point I have to wonder: which way exactly? Do they mean Piet circa 1935, when there were many white helpers but just one in blackface? Do they mean pre-1850, when Piet was more pagan and dark for the winter solstice? Or are they for some reason fanatically focused on that one 1850 version? They need Zwarte Piet to be Jan Schenkman's artwork for *Sinterklaas and His Servant,* in which Zwarte Piet is depicted as a slave. Then again, I have to remember – it could be worse. In Germany, Sinterklaas' helper is called Krampus, and he looks like a death metal entry to the Eurovision Song Contest.

IT'S NOT YOUR FAULT

I've received so many online comments, some that display such a tortured logic it's actually quite impressive. For example:

"Yes, they are slaves, but Sinterklaas freed the slaves, and that's why they serve him – out of gratitude!"

"If we change Zwarte Piet, then what's next? You're going to want to have Black Sinterklaas?"

"Zwarte Piet isn't what you think – it's from the card game where, if you get the *Zwarte Piet,* it means you're a loser. But that said – everybody loves Zwarte Piet!"

I decided to sift through the online comments until I could find the source of the disconnect: "Blackface is only racist in America!"

"Anti-racists are just as racist as racists."

"We'll eliminate Sinterklaas, when you give up fat Santa. Merry Christmas, numb nuts."

Not helpful.

And then there was this one:

"I do mind being called racist for having fond memories of Zwarte Piet."

Helpful!

After figuratively watching a million monkeys typing at a million keyboards, this comment is like finding Shakespeare. And on behalf of the international community, may I hereby declare: "I do not think you are racist for having fond memories of Zwarte Piet as a child." Or – as your therapist might say – "It's not your fault." And let me join in by also confessing that – yes! – the American Santa I grew up with is way too fat. He was super-sized in a 1931 ad campaign to help Coca Cola sell more sugar water. Ever since then Santa is two Christmas cookies away from diabetes.

But then comes another comment with a desperate attempt at *What-about-ism*:

"Santa Claus is helped by elves who are very small people. Is this not equally discriminatory to little people?" Good question! Indeed, it could be discriminatory – if the costume went out of its way to mimic and mock little people. So IF your idea of an 'elf' costume involves kneeling with shoes on your knees, then YES, that would be offensive.

In fact, let's play out this thought exercise: What if Santa's helpers would be based on a particular ethnic stereotype? What if it was a Dutch stereotype? What if every year Americans dressed up as a cartoonish version of how Americans see Dutch people? With no chins and huge foreheads and big, square horse teeth? What if we gave this character a cheerful name like 'Buck-Tooth Dutchie' and made it dance around like Dutch dressage champion Anky van Grunsven? (Dressage involves dressing in formalwear and trying to stay on your horse after giving it a space cake.) Then yes. That would be discriminatory.

MULTI-CULTI PIET

Back in 2012, Quinsy Gario concluded his event by demanding that Dutch leaders admit Zwarte Piet is racist. Eight years later, Prime Minister Mark Rutte came pretty close. During the Dutch #BlackLivesMatter protests, Rutte appeared in a Parliamentary debate and said his perspective on Zwarte Piet had undergone 'major changes.' This is from the man who made a campaign ad in 2017 saying, 'Celebrating Sinterklaas doesn't make you racist.' For a long time, Mark Rutte's attitude was like my wife's had been: "I thought we exported all our racism to America when we sold them the slaves."

In 2020, Prime Minister Rutte told parliament: "I was part of the group that said Zwarte Piet is Black. I've said it often enough here."

[Rutte literally said it In 2014, at the Hague Nuclear Security Summit: "Black Piet is Black, and I can't change that." He said this while hosting Barack Obama. And he could have stopped there, but he continued.

"...In fact, my friends in the Dutch Antilles, they are very happy when they have Sinterklaas because they don't have to paint their faces." And he could have stopped there, but he continued.

"...And when I'm playing Black Piet, I'm for days trying to get off the stuff from my face." The only part he left out was, "Barack, *amirite*?"]

Prime Minister Rutte told parliament: "I have met many people with dark skin, who said they feel discriminated against because Zwarte Piet is Black. And that is the last thing that we want during the Sinterklaas celebrations." Yes, protests really work. Apparently, Mark Rutte took a good long look in the mirror – and saw a little bit of blackface still hiding there.

After Rutte's statement to parliament, US civil rights leader Jesse Jackson wrote an open letter to the Prime Minister, asking for an official end to

Zwarte Piet – the *existence* of Zwarte Piet. Previously, Rev. Jackson had only objected to the *appearance* of Zwarte Piet. I was there in 2009, when Jackson spoke at a packed theater and was asked about Zwarte Piet. I was there thinking, "Here we go! This is the guy who marched with Dr. King! If anybody is going to call out Zwarte Piet for being offensive, it's him." Jackson replied, "I've looked into the hearts of Dutch people, and I have to take into consideration that they are some of the most tolerant, most integrated, most interracial people I've ever seen. And so – when Dutch people say they don't mean it to be racist – I believe they do not mean it to be racist. . . . But the afro and the big lips have got to go."

Attacking the *existence* of Zwarte Piet has proven to be counterproductive. In 2013, the UN's Verene Shepherd referred to the tradition of Zwarte Piet as 'colonial.' She then suggested that the Netherlands drop the entire Sinterklaas tradition in favor of Christmas – which is technically her culture asserting dominance over another culture – which is by definition 'colonial.' The Dutch backlash to Shepherd's statement was intense. It was a perfect example of 'Dutch people do not like being told what to do.' She may as well have said, "From now on, you all have to be Catholic."

By now, soot has replaced blackface in major cities. Blackface is not so visible on TV. Will it be enough? At least the conversation is progressing. It's slowly unifying the nation like both hemispheres of the Dutch brain.

I realize there are still Dutch people who find this topic to be upsetting. As Zwarte Piet fans continue to point out, the original Sinterklaas was not even Dutch. Saint Nicholas came from Myra in Turkey. And if Sinterklaas' boat is supposed to come from Spain, then the dark-skinned Spaniards aboard are Moors, as in 'from Morocco.' So – however you feel about Zwarte Piet – don't forget that the biggest holiday of the Dutch calendar is actually being run by a Turkish guy and a bunch of Moroccans.

CHAPTER 14
DUTCH HONESTY and Dutch Courage

"World Music. Worst music in the world."
– Hans Teeuwen, to a World Music choir

Dutch people are known for being 'direct' – which is an indirect way of saying 'rude.' Welcome to the land where there's no filter! Yes, it takes some getting used to, but it's not categorically bad. If Americans have a reputation for being politely indirect, and the British have a reputation for being politely indecipherable, Dutch people pride themselves on being brutally honest – sometimes at the expense of politeness, or tact, or respect for human dignity. It's like the tale of *The Emperor's New Clothes*. In the Emperor's court, the Americans would say, "Your new clothes look awesome!" The British would say, "It is better to have clothes than to *not* have clothes." And the Dutch would say, "The Emperor is naked! Also, I can see the Emperor's penis. Also, it is a tiny penis."

Yes, Americans will ask, "How are you?" But we don't really care. For fun, you can honestly tell Americans how you're feeling and watch as we react, dumbfounded at the truth. When I visit the states, and my kids say, "I'm going to the toilet," my father will say, "TMI! Too much information." When my father visits the Netherlands and says, "I'm going to the bathroom," my kids say, "Good luck taking a bath in there…" And at work, if your colleague goes on a diet and loses a couple kilos, most people would say, "Wow, have you lost weight?" Whereas your Dutch colleague will say, "Wow, you used to be so fat."

Part of the Dutch motto '*Doe normaal*' seems to mean 'Keep it real,' or 'Call it like you see it.' And the longer I live in the Netherlands, the more I realize what *doe normaal* actually means. It really does mean you should just be yourself. But – if you ever try over-inflating yourself or putting on airs – there's a kind of built-in Dutch bullshit detector that will kick in and cut you off at the knees. It's those Calvinistic roots that are still on display. If you're ever caught bragging, you'll quickly find yourself in a traditional Dutch game I call 'Lobsters in a Basket.' The rules are simple: If you try to climb out of the basket, the others drag you back down.

Before living in the Netherlands, I spent most of my time living in Chicago and New York. In Chicago people care about your past, in New York it's about the future and in the Netherlands it's a mix of both.

In Chicago: "You're from _____? I've been there. Wanna hang out?"

In New York: "You're from _____? I don't care. What's your plan to get rich & famous?"

In the Netherlands: "You want to be rich & famous? Cut the shit! Where are you from? Chicago? Too cold! Plus, here's my favorite insult about Chicago: You are a gangster with guns and bad schools! Why don't you laugh?"

I've had this conversation with Dutch people more than once, after a show: "Hey, I saw you onstage! You are not very funny. Are you really from America? I thought so. You're so loud! And you don't know anything about the rest of the world. You look angry. Do you want to shoot me? You Americans, always shooting each other. Bang bang! …Why don't you laugh?"

Seth Meyers likes to tell the story of a Dutch man who came up to him after the show and said, "Can I buy you a beer? Here. You know, you were not very funny. But – just because you're not funny – doesn't mean you don't deserve a beer." As it happens, that guy was nothing compared to Seth's own dad, Larry Meyers. Mr. Meyers has seen many a Boom

Chicago show, and he is never shy about offering his opinion afterward: "Not your best show tonight! Some of those jokes were stink-o! You've either got to add some punch lines or let 'em go. Great to see you!" In Amsterdam, he fits right in.

When I meet Dutch people after a show, it's often as if they want to show off some new Truth Serum they just drank, combined with Tourette's Syndrome. "Your nose is big!" "Your suit doesn't fit right." "You look Jewish!" And here is a quote which was aimed at a female colleague of mine: "You looked really nice onstage tonight! My friend and I were looking at your trousers, and we made a bet: I'm pretty sure you shave your pubes, but my friend says no, you don't. So, can you help settle our bet? Which is it?" By the way, my female colleague was lesbian. I'm not sure when she officially decided this, but that may have been the moment.

Dutch Honesty can be hard to handle. But when it's combined with Dutch Courage (alcohol), it can be a deadly combination. In America there's the phrase 'Never discuss politics in mixed company.' In the Netherlands, expect uninvited political commentary in the first two minutes of any conversation.

In the days following 9/11, I was here in Amsterdam. A couple times, after I'd do a show, there would be a Dutch guy who wanted to talk to me:

Him: "Are you really American?"

Me: "Yeah."

Him: "Terrible what happened in New York."

Me: "Yeah."

Him: "Let me buy you a drink."

Me: "Thanks."

Him: "*Proost.* (sip) You know, you Americans really did have it coming."

Me: [Spitting my beer]

Him: "Oh yeah… the US had it coming. Who gave the Afghan rebels their weapons? America. Who created the Wahhabi terrorists by propping up the oppressive Saudi regime? The Bush family."

The problem was: I agreed with the argument. But if I'd have said it, they'd have called me a terrorist. In retrospect, I wish there had been more drunk Dutch guys in the Bush White House.

Perhaps the best example of Dutch directness I've encountered was the time I got yelled at by Dutch comedian Hans Teeuwen. If possible, do not get in an argument with Hans Teeuwen. I learned this lesson the hard way.

Hans Teeuwen is known in the Netherlands and the UK for being one of the most politically incorrect voices in comedy. Onstage and off, he is an advocate of free speech. And he practices what he preaches.

I once saw Hans Teeuwen give a TEDx talk on free speech, in which he demonstrated his point by making fun of everyone else onstage before him. He commented on sustainability by smoking a cigarette onstage and saying, "Wouldn't it be great if my cigarette could last forever?" And then he went to the piano. He did a parody of World Music: "The worst kind of music in the world." He described most World Music as "just a bunch of Africans chanting." It was especially awkward because the act that was on right before him was an African choir. More awkward was that they had to come on again after he was done. Afterward, I interviewed him for my blog: "Is that why you took the gig, to make a point about freedom of speech?" He replied, "Nah, I just did it for the money." To this day – as an American – I'm not sure if he was being ironic.

Months later, Hans was developing a new solo show. I'd heard of a great open-mic space for try-outs, so I called him up to tell him about it. It was a Sunday, and he picked up right away. He didn't say much and let me talk. He continued to not say much…

And then he broke in, "Wait a moment, Mr. Shapiro. Is this the same Mr. Shapiro I spoke to after TEDx? The same Mr. Shapiro who was trashing me online?"

My jaw dropped. My testicles retracted. I don't know if it's possible to turn deep red through the phone, but I tried my best.

I had no idea Hans had read my blog! (Did anyone?) He spelled it out for me: "Oh, I know what you were doing, Shapiro. You were just trying to kiss up to the do-gooder crowd and kiss their sweet, influencer asses. You thought that by trashing me you could make a better name for yourself, Shapiro. Well, you didn't think I'd read that shit, did you? But I did! And now you're feeling pretty awkward, aren't you? *Aren't you?!*"

Clearly, Hans was enjoying himself. I could hear him smile as he spoke. He was on a roll. Even as I cringed in agony, I could tell I'd earned myself a custom-made mini-performance. It was like finding an insult comedian and pissing him off, just to hear him rant about you. I concluded the conversation by again offering a tryout space if he needed it. He replied, "No, I knew right away I don't need the space, thanks. I just wanted to make you feel shitty. Okay, bye!"

Dutch honesty. The freedom of speech can and will be used against you. But at least they try to be equal opportunity offenders.

CHAPTER 15

DUTCH CITIZENSHIP
Stump the Dutchie

'The Netherlands is one of the most densely populated countries in the world.'

– My Dutch citizenship course

'The Netherlands is the 24th most densely populated country in the world.'

– Wikipedia

The Dutch citizenship course is essential for teaching Dutch things about Dutch culture that most Dutch people don't know at all. Soon after I started taking classes, I was able to play the game called 'Stump the Dutchie.' Why was the Treaty of Westphalia so important to the Dutch? (My wife wasn't sure.) Who was Johan Thorbecke? (Most Dutch people near Rembrandtplein think he's the patron saint of alcohol poisoning.) What's the most densely populated country in Europe? (It's not Nederland.)

It took me years of kicking and screaming through various Dutch language courses, but I eventually ended up in *Nederlands als Tweede Taal, Niveau 4*. And I received a certificate saying I am an effective Dutch speaker – even though it was barely true. I was the only tall, white male in my citizenship class. I was surrounded by people from Turkey, from Morocco, from Sub-Saharan Africa, Russia, Poland, and Romania. They were, according to a friend of mine, "A United Nations of countries the Dutch government doesn't want here."

After taking the citizenship course, I'm still not sure if I'm an *expat* – or an *allochtoon*. As an American, I'm technically *allochtoon*. As I understand it, '*allochtoon*' is a word Dutch people made up so that – if you don't say it right – they know you're probably 'not from around here.' I was introduced to the term *allochtoon* by a Dutch person, who explained, "It's the opposite of *autochtoon*." Hence 'not one of us.' For a country based on tolerance and civil liberties, Dutch culture is quite creative in pointing out people who are different.

Then there's the term *expat*. I was talking with the director of Amsterdam's Expat Center about the expat tax incentive, 'the 30% rule.' The government wanted to scrap the rule, saying that internationals don't need such an incentive. The Expat Center director went to talk to his bosses in Den Haag to complain. Apparently, they were under the impression that most 'expats' are Shell employees on expense accounts, spending half the year in Singapore and playing golf. Well, in that case I'm less *expat* and more *allochtoon*.

Apparently, the Dutch government is always on the lookout for 'Benefit Tourism,' aka 'Welfare Tourism,' aka immigrants who move here and sponge off the system. And – since they don't really exist – it's very hard to find them! Study after study shows that immigrants pay more into the system than they take out. The Dutch statistics bureau CBS regularly reports that most Europeans in the Netherlands are supporting themselves, thank you very much. Of the 600,000 non-Dutch Europeans who live in the Netherlands, only 6,000 live on welfare. That's 1%. Then there's the other 1%, aka the Top 1%, aka the ones who like the Netherlands because it's a tax haven. I'll let you decide who's the tax problem here.

Dutch society is all about business, and the fact is we immigrants are great for business! Maybe that's why the Dutch Prime Minister ran his re-election campaign with a huge ad saying, 'If you don't like it here, get out.' Especially in campaign season, Dutch politicians love demonizing *allochtonen.* It always feels like the end of a Scooby-Doo episode: "I admit it! I was trying to scare everyone, so they'd stay away!"

Luckily, not all Dutch conservatives think the same way. I was hosting an event once at Randstad recruiting. The main speaker, Ton Hopmans, had a wake-up call for the Dutch government: "The Dutch workforce is dying!" And it's a well-known fact: the Dutch population is getting older, having less babies, and shrinking. The Dutch call it *vergrijzing* – literally 'The Greying.' According to Hopmans, by the year 2030 – probably sooner – every country in Western Europe will be "competing for immigrants. Not kicking them out; *inviting them in.*" As I see it, there's only one solution to *vergrijzing.* It's called *verbruining:* The 'Browning.'

Amsterdam is already nicely diverse. I was watching a speech by the Amsterdam Mayor, who said there are more nationalities represented in Amsterdam than in any other city in the world (even Manhattan). (Manhattan, which has the United Nations…) According to the Mayor, there are 180 nationalities living In Amsterdam. In fact, I've seen one study reporting 179 nationalities, while a different study found 181. Maybe they're both correct. Maybe there's one guy from Burkina Faso, who's dating someone from Uruguay. But she lives in Utrecht. So when he stays over at her place, it's 179. But when she stays at his place, it's 181.

One of the biggest lessons I learned in the citizenship course wasn't about Dutch culture. It was about the other cultures. Every week, we'd find a partner and talk in Dutch about where we were from. I learned that the women in headscarves from Turkey had been to university in Istanbul, and they'd come over together to look for work / further their studies. I learned that the guy from Africa wanted to study water engineering here and then return home to teach. I learned that the Moroccan woman wanted to start up a club for other Moroccan women to do fitness together. Most of them had already heard about the Dutch history of tolerance and immigration. In fact, that's why many of us moved here.

'HEADSCARF IS A SYMBOL OF OPPRESSION'

Our instructor was teaching us about the all-important Western values, such as the Freedom of Religion. That's when we learned that the headscarf is a symbol of oppression. We learned this while I was sitting next to six different women in headscarves. Awkward. One of the women raised her hand and said, "Excuse, please. But – so you know – where I grew up, in Turkey, it was a very secular society. Government rules were very strict. No headscarf allowed. So – for me – to move to the Netherlands and wear my headscarf, that is actually a symbol of liberation."

The response: "Sorry, that is incorrect. If they ask you in the exam, just say it's a symbol of oppression."

And then there was this question: "You are walking down the street and your girlfriend receives unwelcome attention from another man, what do you do?
A Let her solve it herself
B – Both ignore it
C – He gets a smack – and she does too!"

The correct answer is apparently B. But thank you, Dutch government, for assuming that I might want to hit my girlfriend. In class, I suggested the most Dutch answer would be: D – charge him money. I think I was penalized one point for that. But it was worth it.

CHAPTER 16

DUTCH MELTING POT
Multi-Culti Nightmare

"Nederland has become a multi-culti nightmare."

– Geert Wilders

My neighborhood in Amsterdam is nicely diverse, and I love it. I live in the Old West of Amsterdam. My American friends like to tease me: "You live in The Old West? Are there gunfights at high noon?" I tell them, "No, that's '*Nieuw West*…"

(Kidding! There are also no gunfights in *Nieuw West*. But there are a lot of people named *Shariff*.)

Previously, I've lived in Dutch neighborhoods where the old white folks were getting older and the young immigrants were getting younger. So I adopted a Goldilocks approach: "This neighborhood feels too homogenous; this one feels just right." Meanwhile, there are some bleached-blond Goldilocks politicians who have a different strategy: keep out everyone who doesn't also have Goldilocks. But it's not very Dutch.

Nederland has always been a melting pot, and I like to think my neighborhood is a perfect example. On my street, I see Muslim women wearing 'the *hijab*,' and I see Dutch women wearing 'the *rain-scarf*.' The only difference is the rain-scarf doesn't double as a hands-free headset. Yes, there is a steady increase in immigrants – but the clear majority is still 'the blank people.' Or – as the Dutch call them – The Dutch.

I live next to a German artist, a Moroccan civil servant, a Pakistani taxi driver, a Turkish social worker, an Indonesian architect, a Surinamese deliveryman, an Italian telemarketer, an African city worker, a Ukrainian klezmer musician, and a Dutch film editor with a stutter. And the only one I have a problem with is the one who doesn't clean up after their dog.

One of the more recent arrivals in my neighborhood is a Russian guy, and he loves it that there's an American nearby. He announces it loudly whenever he sees me. "Here comes the crazy American." "Look, it's the crazy American!" And: "Look out, he's so crazy." I asked him one day what he meant, and he explained, "Grigory, you must realize that – to be American – you are by definition crazy. You are taught that 'Life is Perfect,' and it must become more perfect as you go on. This is crazy. In Russia we are taught 'Life is a series of one disaster after another.' ... And we are never disappointed."

And then it occurred to me – in terms of national stereotypes – these are the extremes: America ("Yay!") and Russia ("Aww..."). And then right in the middle there's the Dutch ("Meh...").

Now if I'm being honest, yes – there are some troublemakers in my neighborhood. See if you can guess who's the biggest problem.

THE DUTCH GUY NEXT DOOR

Ronald was a Dutchman, who moved in to the rental building next door. We weren't clear on what kind of disability he had, but you could tell life hadn't been treating him well. In his thirties, he looked like he was already in his fifties. Stubble on his face and stubble on his bald-ish head. He had sunken, dark eyes that darted around with an infectious nervousness. He wore camos & hoodies with an Ajax scarf, dressing as if trying to be accepted as an Ajax hooligan. Whether they would have him or not was unclear.

As soon as he moved in, he began with the charming habit of locking his bike to other people's bikes. It's the worst impression you can make on your new neighbors, but it's a surefire way to get them knocking on your door. Then came the students ringing our doorbell looking for Ronald, since he'd rented them a room in his apartment. Or so they'd thought. Instead, he was taking their security deposit and then refusing to answer his door. Next came the colorful characters who rang our doorbell saying Ronald owed them money, and did we have any cash to cover for our neighbor? That's when *we* stopped answering the door.

Part of Ronald's disability became clear when the fire trucks arrived one evening. Ronald was an epileptic. On the 3rd floor. Every time he'd have a seizure, they'd need the crane from the fire department to airlift him down to the ambulance in the street. And the police car for good measure. Our street was regularly filled with red lights, blue lights, orange too. It was festive, but not very practical.

We neighbors convened a meeting: immigrant & native; renters & owners – and the 'neighborhood coordinator' from the police. We asked, "Who puts an epileptic on the 3rd floor?" We were told that the housing corporation from next door would have to relocate Ronald, but it can take a long time. What sped things up was the night Ronald threatened to set us all on fire. It was after midnight, and Ronald had blockaded his door, smashed out the front window, and yelled down that he was suicidal and opening up the gas valve intending to blow up the building. We watched as the assault team assembled, went in, and brought him out.

And that was the end of Ronald in our neighborhood. At least it was a nice reason to get a bunch of us multi-culti neighbors together. And we agreed: the multi-culti part is not the problem.

THE GERMAN ARTIST & HIS PLANTS

My German neighbor Walter is a tall, skinny, dark-haired artist in his fifties. 'The Fifties' also describes his style of dress: he prefers a fedora hat and a long, wool coat, even in summer. I never see Walter *smoking* a joint, but it's obvious he's a pot-smoker from the amount of vowels he uses to greet me: "Heeeeeey! *Buurmaaaaaaaan*!"

Walter enjoys combining his artistic expression with his green thumb. Our front stoop is cluttered with found objects, converted into planters filled with bamboo and lavender and honeysuckle. And whatever grows naturally, man. Across the street from Walter is a wall covered with ivy all the way up to the roof. At least it was.

One sunny Saturday, an older Dutch couple decided to rip all the ivy down. They said they'd heard complaints that the ivy was damaging their wall. Oddly, it's a rental building, and they had no permission to rip down the ivy. But it's their country, so I guess we'll live with their norms and values: pockmarked gray wall and graffiti. My favorite tag so far: 'Turks, go back to Morocco.'

THE PAKISTANI TAXI DRIVER & HIS WIFE & KID

They live in the apartment next to us. The three of them are squashed into two rooms. Of course, the husband isn't around a lot. He works long hours, and we never see him. They speak Urdu to each other. To us, they speak Dutch. Her Dutch is coming along. Almost as bad as mine.

She is a neighborly neighbor. She loves bringing us food. She'll bring a bowl full of chickpea soup. Or a snack made with crushed pistachios. Or dessert, involving sweet yoghurt and honey and sesame. These are the items I normally wouldn't order from a menu. But they're delicious. And she is not afraid to ring the doorbell – even when it's not a good moment. Now I understand that Dutch exam question.

I wondered aloud to my wife if it might be a good idea to return the favor. She cooked up the idea to cook up something typically Dutch. So I decided on the traditional dish I know best: *Witlof / ham-kaas* – an oven dish featuring potatoes with Belgian endive, covered with ham and cheese.

If you haven't spotted the inherent flaw in this plan, you are like I was. I brought my dish out of the oven and proudly touted it over to the neighbors, ringing the doorbell and offering my gift with gusto. My neighbor took one sniff at it and turned away in disgust: "Is that – pork?"

Yes, I'm the guy who brings a steaming-hot dish full of ham to a Muslim woman's door, as a gesture of thanks. If there is a problem in our neighborhood, perhaps the enemy is us. The good news is: in terms of Dutch culture, I guess I'm fitting right in.

CHAPTER 17
DUTCH EDUCATION
Race to the Middle

"The Dutch education system: VMBO, HAVO & VPRO."

– Overheard at Expat Trade Fair

My two Dutch-American kids go to Dutch public schools, and I wouldn't have it any other way. Mostly because – having looked at the international schools – we couldn't afford it any other way. Dutch schools can be overachievers. They teach kids the things they need to know, as well as things they don't need to know – and even some things they probably shouldn't know. In terms of culture shock, Dutch schools can be 'a learning experience.'

For a country with a reputation for liberalism and tolerance, Nederland's schools offered some odd first impressions – and some were spectacularly awkward. We quickly learned the difference between *black* schools and *white* schools. White schools are for white kids. Black schools are for, well, *other.* "How can this be," I thought. "Can it really be that Dutch schools practice segregation?" Then it was explained to me by other Dutch parents. "No, it's not segregated! There are white kids in the 'black' schools. (It's just that I wouldn't want *my* white kids to join them.)" Maybe not so different from America, after all.

In Dutch primary schools, there are some wonderfully politically incorrect rituals. When there's a birthday, I've encountered a song called 'Hanky Panky Shanghai.' This is a song, to the tune of 'Happy Birthday,'

in which the teachers will make slanty-eyed faces and make the children join in – including the Chinese girl Xiao Xiao – to make sure no one feels left out. Then there's the song about the boy who's so black he needs to carry a parasol in the sun. And don't get me started on Zwarte Piet.

One becomes sensitive to what the little ones are learning, especially when the teachers are making fun of your home country. My kids come home regularly with stories of their Dutch teachers making fun of Americans for overeating. (While this is of course true, I think the jokes are *my* job, okay?.) During a geography lesson, my daughter hears about how Americans don't know much geography. (It's true: in my high school I had driving lessons. Geography was about navigating my way to the mall.) Once – at my daughter's preschool – I was invited to sit in on Song Time for a singalong of '*Berend Botje*.' There's a part at the end with the refrain 'America, America.' And – since this was around the time America had just invaded somewhere – the teacher sang 'America' with a big Thumbs Down gesture, stuck out her tongue, and encouraged the kids to do the same. I mentioned to the teacher later, "You know I'm from America." She said, "I know."

Don't get me wrong. Compared to the United States, I love Dutch schools. In the US, they have Shooter Drills. In the Netherlands, my kids think, 'Shooter Drill' means practicing penalty kicks in the schoolyard. I love that there's not the disparity between rich and poor kids that I grew up with in the US. And I love that the price difference between public and private schools here is not as severe as the US. We were able to start out at a primary school in Amsterdam – which in America would be called 'Waldorf,' and would cost thousands of dollars a year. I like to think the Waldorf school is named after the mixed salad featuring quite a few nuts. The motto of the school was 'Become Who You Are.' In practice, that meant, 'Just Act Normal.'

For me, one of the oddest cultural distinctions of Dutch schools is the latent Calvinism that teaches children 'don't rock the boat.' Yes, the Dutch are a very tolerant people ...as long as you '*doe normaal*.' Just act normal. And it starts when they're young. My daughter started taking ballet lessons and getting good at it. But she seemed to be experiencing resentment, including from her teacher. I asked one of the other parents why this could be happening. I heard: "*Hoge bomen vangen veel wind*," Literally: 'Tall trees catch more wind,' or 'the more you excel, the more resistance you get.' In essence, the lesson seems to be: *Don't try*.

Next, it was at my son's school that I encountered the phrase '*Steek je hoofd niet boven het maaiveld uit (anders wordt 'ie afgehakt)*.' In other words: 'Don't stick your neck out, or your head will be chopped off.'

In America, children grow up with a different type of socialization. We hear phrases like 'Just do it' or even 'Be Best.' And the classic 'The squeakiest wheel gets the oil.' In other words, 'To get the attention you deserve, it helps to be loud and obnoxious.' In Dutch schools, it's: 'Keep your head down, or get decapitated.'

This theme got really interesting when my daughter was offered a spot at the Dutch National Ballet Academy. To accept the spot, she'd have to leave her class early and switch to a different school. My American family reacted with cheers: "That's amazing." Also: "So proud!" And: "Awesome!"

My Dutch family reacted differently: "Uh-oh… that sounds like a big change." Also: "That's a tough business, isn't it?" And: "Are you sure you're not just forcing your dreams on her?" And – yes – these are all questions we'd asked ourselves as parents. But the fact was our daughter had already spent too much time feeling underwhelmed by her old class. She demanded more challenging coursework, more stimulation, more education. So she moved. We'd bump into the parents from the old school, and they'd ask about my daughter. At first, I'd tell them the truth: "It's fine, she's having a great time!" And they would look disappointed. Then I tried telling them "It's heavy. Lots of work. Really hard on her." And they'd say, "Ooh! Tell me more!"

My son experienced 'Just act normal' from a different angle, by developing a chronic illness as a teenager. The school system's response was basically: "Wouldn't it be more convenient if he didn't have this condition?" A few years before my son's diagnosis, the Dutch education system underwent a big change. I remember I was hired to perform at an event for school administrators, where the theme was 'We're removing the stigma of the term *Special Needs Child*. From now on, we'll treat all the kids the same!' One of the school administrators asked, "What about the kids who really do have special needs?" And the organizers pledged that they'd feel more 'normal' this way.

Yes, there are benefits to acting like everything is normal. But as soon as there are exceptions to the norm, Dutch schools can develop their own set of symptoms. At my son's school, the mentor said, "Yes, your son can miss some of his classes." Then the next day the academic coordinator called up threatening him for missing classes. Can he change the date of some of exams, due to doctor visits? "Yes, of course!" But the next day: "No, it's not possible." At one point, the academic coordinator explained: "Now that class sizes are bigger due to all the formerly special needs kids, the teachers are feeling overwhelmed with all the exceptions." So yes, in Nederland they believe that 'Children are the Future,' but teachers have a permanent contract.

When it comes down to it, we've learned the most valuable lesson: even when you're sick, just act normal.

CHAPTER 18

DUTCH SERVICE
An Oxymoron

"The Dutch are historically a non-hierarchical society. Since they overthrew the Spanish in the 1500s, they make it a point not to take orders from anyone."

– Ton Heibergs, Royal Tropical Institute

No, Dutch people don't like taking orders from anyone. This includes waiters in many Dutch restaurants. In the Netherlands, they say, "The client is King." Specifically, the Spanish king they overthrew in the 1500s.

Only in Dutch restaurants have I had this conversation.

Me: "Check, please?"

Waiter: (cleaning behind the bar, avoiding eye contact)

Me: "Hello, could we have the bill, please?"

Waiter: (going for smoke break, avoiding eye contact)

Me: "Please, can we pay?"

Waiter: (eventually delivers the check)

Me: "Finally… we could have walked out about three times by now."

Waiter: (angrily) "Well, why didn't you, then?!"

The term 'Dutch service' can be an oxymoron.

Where do Dutch people learn their customer service skills? There's actually quite a lot of training for the hospitality industry. For example, there's the Hotel School in Amsterdam West. It's the one where the smoking area is located right outside the front entrance. So for anyone passing by, it appears that an integral part of Dutch service training is SMOKE BREAK.

The very term 'Dutch hospitality' can get you into trouble. Even when people invite you over, it's by appointment only. I've met Dutch people who say, "You simply must come visit!" But make sure you don't drop in unannounced. When I first arrived in Nederland, I took up my neighbor's offer to drop by sometime, but they were about to have dinner. "No problem," he said. "While we're eating our dinner, you can sit in the other room and read a magazine. Smells good, huh?"

The concept of tipping is quite different in America and the Netherlands too. One of our favorite places in the Netherlands is Café Restaurant Amsterdam. We'll frequently go there after returning from the States. Our servers are attentive and work as a team. When we ate there last, I was paying the bill, and my American tipping instincts took over:

"15% of 68 euros is upwards of € 10. So I'll give 80 euros to be safe."

My Dutch wife protested, "No! They'll think you're trying to be some kind of rich, showoff, *uitslover*. Just round up!"

"Fine, I said. 'I'll give 70."

"Perfect."

"Are you sure? Two euros tip on a bill of € 68?"

And – sure enough – when I gave the two euros, they looked genuinely surprised and said, "Thank you!"

Whereas – in America – they'd have tried to claw my eyes out.

RETAIL FAILS

In America, the sales stereotype is 'ABC: Always Be Closing.' In Nederland, it's just a bit different.

My wife got a gift coupon to shop at a *parfumerie*. It was full of 'handmade scents' and little cards for spraying and testing the perfumes. After a few minutes, the shopkeeper came up and said, "Can't you spray that outside? I have to work here all day, and it gives me a headache!" It was suggested that perhaps the woman might want to find another place to work. As it turned out, she didn't just work in the shop. She was the owner.

A friend of mine was trying on boots in Den Haag. She finally found the pair she was looking for, but the man behind the counter announced, "We're almost closed." My friend asked if she could just check if they had the right size? The shopkeeper returned with the boots, and my friend went to try them on. She began taking off her shoes and trying on the boots, but apparently she wasn't quick enough, as the shopkeeper turned off the lights.

"We're closing," he said.

"Uh-oh," my friend said. "I guess I'll quickly try on the other boot…"

"I said we're closed," said the man.

My friend protested, "What if I just pay for them right now?"

"Sorry. The cash register is shut down."

"But I want to buy the boots."

"Then you should have come earlier," he said. And he kicked her out of the shop. Sometimes making a sale is not as important as making a customer suffer.

By now, there are signs of improvement. These days, a glass of tap water will be provided free of charge at the café. Not long ago, tap water was inexplicably off-limits. Possibly poisonous! And definitely conducive to eye daggers. The new generation of Dutch service staff seem to care a bit more about their work. And I've personally given 'Customer Friendliness' trainings to Schiphol Duty Free staff. (But I can't vouch for any results, there.)

One more example: My father was staying at a bed & breakfast in the Jordaan. The owner was apparently a former psychotherapist. This is what my father found out when staying there. My dad reported many interesting chats in the mornings. The owner would put out a traditional Dutch breakfast and just observe my father as he ate. At the end of his

stay, the owner asked my father if he would like to come stay again at the B&B. My father said, "Well, sure, I think I might come back and stay here again." The owner looked him straight in the eye and said, "No you won't." And he was right.

THE AMERICAN ALTERNATIVE

And of course, Dutch people point out the negative stereotypes about American service. Americans say, "Have a nice day" and "How are you doing?" And we don't really care. But there's one thing worse. When we actually DO care.

I was back in the US for a mini family reunion. It was a theme restaurant outside Chicago with my dad and my brothers, whom I hadn't seen in two years. We got a back room all to ourselves, which was great. The only problem was a little attention-starved freak called our waitress.

"Hi! My name is Ariel, and I'll be your server today! If there's anything you need at any point, feel free to let me know. Would you like to hear our specials today?"

"No," I said.

"Okay, well, here they are anyway..." And she went on to tell us the whole menu.

We ordered as quickly as possible, so I could catch up with my brothers. One of them is a screenwriter in LA. I asked, "Is it true your script is getting financed? And you're going to direct? I want to hear more!"

And here was Ariel again: "Did you guys want to order any extra fries or side dishes at this time?"

"No, thank you." Anyway, my brother was already doing some casting for the movie, and he was getting some interest from some big names.

Ariel: "Do you guys want any refills?"

The drinks were enormous already. I felt like I was getting sick just looking at the cola.

"No thank you." My brother told me that it's an Oscar winner who wants to star in his movie. Who was it!?

Ariel again: "I went ahead and brought you guys some more drinks just in case. Let me just make some room for you..."

And I was the one who decided to use my Dutch bluntness. I said, "You know what? We don't want drinks right now. We just want the chance to finish our conversation. I don't know if you can tell, but we're having a little family reunion."

Ariel chimed in, "OH! Family reunion! That's nice. My family is all from right around here, so we see each other constantly. I guess you could say we have a family reunion all the time. My brother says he wants to go away to school..."

I couldn't believe it. Why did she think I wanted to skip hearing about my own family, so I could hear about hers? I said, "Sorry – maybe I've been unclear. I don't get to see these guys very often. I live in Amsterdam." Big mistake. Ariel continued, "OH! Amsterdam! I'd love to go to Amsterdam. Because that's my name: ARIEL! And I have to go see that statue of the Little Mermaid, in Amsterdam."

Part of me wanted to correct her, but the other part of me had to admit: I was dying to get back to Dutch service. I was dying to ask for a drink and have the waiter tell me to f*ck off.

THAT IS NOT POSSIBLE

There's something about Dutch service that I've found to be integral to the Dutch experience. I remember the day I had this realization. It was when we had to get a new washing machine.

Here's the story. Our old washing machine broke down. So we went to the white good store (*de witgoed shop*). We shopped around for different brands, and we ended up doing what every good Dutch couple does: we bought a German machine. It was the heaviest.

We told them at the store: "Installing it may be tricky. It's going to have to go past the bathtub, over a toilet, into a little nook."

"No problem!" was the answer. "They will even take the old one away. That is the job of our service team."

SERVICE TEAM. When I hear this term in the Netherlands, it sets off warning bells and red flags. When *service* and *team* appear in the same sentence, it usually means trouble.

We were told it should be possible. It sounded good enough. So the service team showed up. And they realized our washing machine is not easy to get to. It lives in the back corner of our bathroom. We actually have a bathtub and a toilet in the same room, which is not common. And then, when the service team surveyed the scene, we heard that classic Dutch phrase, "Mmmm. That is not possible." This means "It is possible, I just don't feel like it."

My first instinct was to play the role of the self-righteous American: "They said at store it should be possible!"

But then it struck me: “Wait a minute – no. Maybe it’s more Dutch to relate to each other in a different way.” I told my wife, “Stand back, honey. I’m going to try to communicate with them.”

She said, “Please don’t try to do it in Dutch.”

I slumped myself down next to the delivery guys and said, “Wow, this sucks for you. Big heavy washing machine. You guys have to lift it up and then over and then down. You have to lift heavy stuff all day. Don’t you? Yeah. Must be tough. You know, they said at the store that it would be possible. But I see now that it is not possible. So I guess, okay, you can go. I guess I’ll just have to do it myself. I might hurt my back. So I could call a neighbor. But what if he gets hurt, then I need insurance, which I don’t have. So maybe just take it back to the truck. You’ll just have to return it…”

And they looked at each other, as if to say: “Wow. That was really good complaining.”

And then they said, “Well, okay, we’ll give it a try…”

And sure enough: Presto! It was done.

That’s how to really communicate the Dutch way. And they don’t teach you that in the citizenship class.

CHAPTER 19
DUTCH MOVIES
How the Dutch See Themselves

"Film is [a country's] ideology at its purest."
– Slavoj Žižek, philosopher

I dreamt I was in a crappy movie with Naomi Watts… no wait, that really happened. But I'll get to that next.

One of the first Dutch films I ever saw was an art house film in Chicago: *Spoorloos* ('Without a Trace'). *Spoorloos* is a movie, featuring a mild-mannered Dutchman who is also a sadistic killer. It was a very good first impression.

In America, we like our happy endings, even if it means a tacked-on, Hollywood ending. Dutch movies don't have happy endings; Dutch movies just end. Boy meets Girl, Boy loses Girl, Boy and Girl get together for obligatory nude scene and have sex anyway. "Do they live happily ever after?" Probably not.

Spoorloos – the movie is even better. [Spoiler Alert: I'm about to give away the ending to this movie you may have seen ages ago and don't quite remember.]

It's about a guy whose wife gets kidnapped. Actually, it's not his wife. They're just 'living together,' because it's Nederland. Boy meets Girl, Boy loses Girl, Boy goes crazy looking for Girl. And he finally meets the guy who kidnapped her. He's this creepy Dutch family man with a pointy beard.

Pointy Beard says, "You want to know what happened to your girlfriend? Well, I can't tell you. But I can show you." The boyfriend is so desperate he says *yes*. He lets himself be drugged, and the screen goes black. The next thing we see is a lighter in the darkness. *Flick, flick*. And we hear the sound of dirt being shoveled onto a coffin. Our hero is being buried alive, just like his girlfriend. The end.

I'd never seen a movie like this before! In fact, it was a bit of a hit in America – because of the ending. Lots of people were talking about the film, saying, "Wow, the Dutch are hard core." And of course, not long after, there was a Hollywood remake: *The Vanishing* with Kiefer Sutherland. It's a lot like watching any episode of *24* with Jack Bauer. He's desperate, looking for clues, torturing people. And then he meets the kidnapper (played by Oscar-winner Jeff Bridges) (whose Dutch accent wins the award for 'Worst-Ever').

[Spoiler Alert: the rest is the same, shot by shot.] Our hero drugs himself, wakes up in a box, and flicks on his lighter. The only difference is it's America, so they had to use a big Zippo lighter.

But Hollywood did it – they killed the hero. Hard core! Then they tried the film in front of American test audiences, and the Americans didn't get it. They said, "But… how does he get out of the box?"

The producers explained: "That's the whole point: he doesn't. Surprise!"

The test audiences still didn't get it: "But seriously, when does he get out of the box?"

"He doesn't! There is no happy ending. It's a testament to the desperation of the human condition."

"Oh, okay. … But can't you make it so he gets out of the box?"

So – of course – they filmed an alternate ending. Kiefer Sutherland is in the box. Jeff Bridges finishes shoveling the dirt on the box. Cut to a new girlfriend who for some reason is driving around in the woods. Suddenly, she stops: "Is that shoveling I hear?" She rushes into the middle of the forest and somehow, in the dark, she detects freshly turned earth. Then she's digging up our hero, she pries open the box, and there he is! ...But she's too late. He's already dead. Or is he? Our hero wakes up with a huge breath of relief and hugs his new girlfriend. Happy ending!

But wait – here comes the bad guy. He's got a shovel and wants to kill our hero. So they shoot him, and he's dead. Or is he? Just as they hug again, the killer wakes up and grabs the girlfriend, so that Kiefer Sutherland has to whack him with the shovel. He smashes Jeff Bridges' head in, drops the shovel and literally has to look into the camera and say, "It's over... It's over." That's what it took for the American test audience to finally be satisfied: "Okay! I guess it's over."

Of course, for the Dutch market – if they would have filmed a separate ending – the hero would have killed the bad guy, had sex with his girlfriend and then died. "Do they live happily ever after? Probably not."

AMERICAN LIFE IMITATES DUTCH ART

One way to find out how a culture sees itself is to look at its cinema and directors. In the case of the Netherlands, the best-known directors seem like they're trying to be American. Jan de Bont made his US debut with *Speed*, a veritable homage to the Hollywood action movie. Paul Verhoeven moved to the US and made *Robocop*, which mixed a lot of social commentary into the sci-fi action movie genre. That plus Verhoeven's sci-fi dystopia films *Total Recall* and *Starship Troopers* spelled out a Dutchman's view of the future: "Will things get better? Probably not."

And next up for US success was supposed to be Dutch writer-director Dick Maas. Dick Maas is a mystery to me. He has been making American knock-off films since the early '80s. But I can never tell: is it homage or parody? I remember the boat chase in *Amsterdamned,* where the cop chases the serial killer along the famous canals. But after our hero goes crashing into the rowing club, then the Dutch street organ, then an even more implausible brass band flotilla... you're left wondering. Is Maas is taking this seriously or is he taking the piss?

Dick Maas' first-ever movie was *De Lift* in 1983. It was a simple horror story about an elevator where people were being killed – by the elevator. For everyone who's ever wondered what happens when you get your head caught between the elevator doors, this movie is for you. For many Dutch people, Dick Maas is like the Dutch Ed Wood. His films are 'so bad they're good.'

In the year 2000, it was time for Dick Maas to make his big jump to the US market. He decided to redo his first movie, *De Lift,* with a *Die Hard* makeover. The exteriors were filmed in Manhattan, but the bulk of the production took place in Almere (by the *Big Brother* studios). And I went to the audition. Everyone from Boom Chicago tried out for the film. Ike Barinholtz got to play a fussy office assistant. Josh Meyers was on a SWAT team. And I got a role as a tech nerd / computer expert named Chip. (Get it?)

The next thing I knew I was on set, next to Naomi Watts – and Dick Maas! Now I would finally find out: are we taking this seriously or going for comedy? Am I playing this mystery like *X-Files,* or like *Scooby Doo*? Dick Maas – being Dutch – put the *direct* in 'director.' He was very up-front about what he wanted from the scene and what the story needed: I had to give the pivotal clue that would set the final act in motion. So, okay – more like *X-Files.* But then he stopped to dictate the details of my nerd costume: mismatched suspenders and tie, goofy glasses, and food stains on my shirt. Clownish. So, okay – *Scooby Doo.* I remember we had to do a retake to make sure there was enough pizza sauce on me. So I played it self-aware / goofy. But Maas said no – play it serious.

Was he being ironic, and I just didn't get it, because I'm American? The truth was still out there. I decided to ask the other actors. At that point, I'd never heard of Naomi Watts. It was the year 2000 – no one had. At that point we were all more impressed with her co-star James Marshall from *Twin Peaks*. James was playing it seriously – very seriously. I joked with him and said he didn't seem as dumb as his character on TV. He eagerly agreed. After *Twin Peaks*, he'd not only had to fight typecasting. He'd had to deal with a serious illness. The Dick Maas movie was to be his comeback and his "big chance to play an intelligent role in a smart script." Clearly, his agent hadn't seen many Dick Maas movies.

As for Naomi Watts, she was playing it seriously too. She had a lot of work to do. From Australia, Naomi had a broad Australian accent – the accent I've heard Australians refer to as 'Strine.' But she was working on her American accent for the film. We'd be running lines, and in a flawless American accent, she'd say, "Chip, do you want a coffee?" And then she'd turn aside and ask, "Dizz thet sound roight?" Thanks to Dick Maas, I'm proud to say I helped Naomi Watts with her American accent. We had a couple scenes together. On camera I played a nerd, and she played a smart, good-looking femme fatale who was way out of my league. Off-camera, our relationship was no different.

By 2001, Dick Maas' serious parody was ready to debut in the US. The movie was called *Down*. It was one of the most remarkable flops ever. Can you guess why? In the script – written by Dick Maas – the killer elevator is now bumping off so many people in Manhattan that the White House calls it 'terrorism' and sends in commandos with 'Stinger' anti-aircraft missiles. Of course, this was standard film script material for every movie that came out after September 11.

But here's the thing: Dick Maas' movie came out *before* September 11. *One week before* – on September 4. For a week, the film did rather well. But somehow, after September 11, no one wanted to see a horror movie set in Manhattan about people dying in skyscrapers.

Say what you want about Dick Maas movies, but he did kind of predict 9/11. Re-watching the film, I couldn't believe some of the dialogue. Of course, Maas needed a missile launcher in his story to set up the obligatory explosion at the end. But how did he justify it? Here's some of the text.

Commando 1: "Why do we need Stingers?"
Commando 2: "Terrorists have airplanes too."

And this bit:

Commando 1: "Up we go."
Commando 2: "If you see Bin Laden, say hello."

Yes, Dick Maas predicted Osama bin Laden would attack skyscrapers in Manhattan. Or – to be more specific – he predicted the Americans would over-react enough to *expect* Osama bin Laden would attack skyscrapers in Manhattan. In retrospect, I wish the US would have taken Dick Maas more seriously.

CHAPTER 20

DUTCH HEALTH CARE

Pain Tolerance

"All the criminals and drug addicts in Europe have gone and exploited the openness in Amsterdam. ...Amsterdam is a mess."

– The O'Reilly Factor, Fox News

"Dutch doctors prescribe the least amount of antibiotics in Europe."

– *De Volkskrant*

There was a famous episode of Bill O'Reilly on Fox News, trashing Amsterdam as some kind of drug-addicted 'Sodom and Gomorrah on the Amstel.' Yet – if that was true – then you could get drugs from, say, the Dutch health care system, which is virtually impossible.

If you watch the news in the US, you may have the idea that the Netherlands has 'socialized medicine.' (It doesn't.) Or that the Dutch have alarmingly high numbers of drug users, drug addicts and drug deaths. (That's the US.) Or that the Dutch are misogynistic and guilty of sexual harassment. (That's specifically Bill O'Reilly.)

My grandpa used to watch Fox News. He'd call us up and ask, "Are you guys safe over there? I hear in Europe you've got socialized medicine.

You can't even see a doctor, if you want to." And that's when I'd have to set the record straight: "Seeing a doctor here is not a problem!" …The problem is getting the doctor to do anything.

Most countries have doctors swear an oath: some version of the Hippocratic oath. In Nederland, there seems to be a different oath: "As much as possible, I will tell my patients 'Why don't you go home and get some rest?'"

It is not uncommon to begin and end your doctor visit like this:

"I have a head cold."

"Why don't you go get some rest?"

"I have a chest cold."

"Why don't you go get some rest?"

"I have a head cold and a chest cold and Covid. Also, my arm was bitten off by a squid."

"…Why don't you go get some rest?"

The frustrating thing for an American is this: often, the advice is absolutely correct. For me, staying home from work and healing myself has worked every time. It was hard at first. I thought, "If I take a sick day, isn't that a sign of weakness? Shouldn't I pump myself full of antibiotics and keep on working?" My wife replied, "And infect everyone else? Only if you are sick in the head. That's so American. Your whole country is addicted to painkillers!"

My wife has such antipathy for drugs she gave birth to two babies with nothing but deep breathing. My family in America still doesn't believe it:

"But when did you have the epidural?"

We didn't.

"But what kind of anesthesia did you use?"

Nothing.

"…Are you guys safe over there?"

Granted, we could have gone for a hospital birth if we'd wanted it. When my wife opted for natural childbirth, that was one of my first questions. Refreshingly, the midwife assured me she was not anti-drug; she was just pro-nature. These Dutch folks are so comfortable with their bodies that they don't even mind using terms like 'shame hair' and 'shame lips' with a straight face. We were told: "If there's anything wrong at any point, that's when we go to the hospital."

My wife and I did end up going to the hospital at one point – which convinced me not to trust the hospital. About a month before the due date of our first child, my wife got a strange feeling. Normally, she'd be feeling the baby move or kick every day. But there were a couple of days in a row that she felt nothing. As a first-time mother, she got super-nervous. So, on a Sunday, we decided to go in to the hospital.

If I can recommend a day of the week to go to a Dutch hospital, I would not recommend a Sunday. Even if my wife had been giving birth, I think they would have asked, "Can you hold it in until tomorrow?" We were told that there was only one obstetrician on duty, and there was another woman in labor, so we'd have to wait. I explained that my wife was super-nervous, and we just needed a consultation. Just someone in a uniform to tell us everything was okay. We waited.

While the obstetrician was busy, we were visited by an obstetrician-in-training. She showed us into a room, and we explained again that we were super-nervous. She made an ultrasound scan of the baby and paused as she held the wand over my wife's belly. Then we got the famous Dutch bedside manner: "Either I'm reading this wrong, or your baby has birth defects. It could be a misshapen head. I'll go get the doctor now (and be gone for as long as possible.)" We were scared stiff.

She literally left me holding the ultrasound wand in my hand. I decided to keep smiling. I thought I'd make the best of it: "What the hell, I'll give myself an ultrasound." I introduced my wife to my food baby. That

helped us calm down a little, but it felt like forever before the proper obstetrician came in. Without a word to us, he instructed the trainee that you're supposed to measure from the outside of the line, not the inside. He left – still without a word to us. The trainee said, "Your baby's fine."

And I felt much better about having the baby at home.

SPEED BABY

Then the day came. The water broke. At this point in the story, my family wanted to know: "How did you get to the hospital?"

We didn't.

"But who delivered the baby?"

The midwife came to us.

"In an ambulance?"

No, in an old Volvo.

"...Are you guys safe over there?"

To tell the truth, we were supposed to go to the hospital. When the water broke it wasn't totally clean, and that means you're supposed to have breathing machines nearby, just in case. I watched as the midwife called the hospital and was told there was no space. Why? It was a Saturday.

The midwife continued dialing. My wife continued dilating. The midwife called another hospital. Again, no space. Finally, she found an open spot at Slotervaart Hospital – a hospital which would later close forever. It was the same hospital that said maybe our baby was deformed. Before I could say, "I'm sure it will be fine…" my wife had dilated to eight centimeters.

The midwife and I looked at each other and silently did the math. To an American, eight centimeters doesn't sound so big. But multiply that times the three flights of stairs we'd have to descend to get to the street. …And then what? I couldn't believe there was no plan for this. We could call an ambulance? Or maybe it would be faster with her Volvo? Or a taxi? I can't believe there was a moment when I honestly thought, "Yes, a taxi might want to take us." For the record, according to the List of Least Desirable Passengers, 'Pregnant Woman' is right up there between 'Vomiting Vagrant' and 'Bleeding Junkie.'

In my desperation, I even thought of using our most common form of transport. Yes, dear reader, there was a moment when I actually considered taking my 8-cm dilated wife on the back of my bike. Of course, I didn't expect she'd ride herself! Somehow, I'd pictured my wife riding side-saddle, with the midwife biking along beside us, yelling, "Pull your knees up! Keep breathing!" And soon I'd be biking three people. What could be more Dutch?

As it turned out, we didn't make it out of the bedroom. The midwife coached my wife through the pain, as it came in waves. She was pain surfing. And then, the next thing I knew, out popped a baby. The midwife said, "Isn't it beautiful?" I thought, "You mean this purple, writhing, alien creature with the rugby ball head?" And then my baby daughter – like a cartoon character who'd just been hit over the head with a frying pan – shook her cranium until her skull popped back into its normal shape. And I thought, "That's my girl."

And that is how we ended up having our first baby at home on our bed. No anesthetic, luckily no complications, and then – as directed – we went and got some rest.

MOTHER COOKIE

Our second baby was an even more all-natural experience. The water broke and again the amniotic fluid wasn't clear. And this time it was a Monday. Surely, we could get to a hospital this time? Not even close. This time, everything went much faster. This time, we used what is called a 'birthing stool,' which allows your baby to be born with the help of gravity. So instead of "Push, push!" our midwife had to say, "Hold it in!"

Our second midwife's name was Door – a perfect name in either language. As the baby was crowning, she was busy with some special pillow. I was standing behind my wife, who was doing her best to slow things down, but at one point, Mother Nature's gravity took over. My wife said, "I can't hold it anymore!" And I could only watch as Door grabbed the pillow and made a diving catch! She went all out. I can still see her diving, in slow motion. And Door – not my baby – hit the floor.

What followed next was a kind of shamanistic gore-fest. The midwife's assistant stepped in and made a whole production out of the afterbirth. With bravado, she said, "Wait, there's more!" And she proceeded to do an imitation of the magician pulling handkerchiefs out of the sleeve. She pulled until she reached the placenta, but no one was there to catch that. The placenta hit the floor, and the blood sprayed all over the walls like a special effect in a horror movie.

The midwife's assistant then gingerly picked up the placenta and cradled it in her arms. It was like a little competition. Midwife Door was with our baby, saying, "Ooh! It's a boy, he's beautiful!" And next to her was the assistant, looking at the placenta, saying, "Ooh! Look at these beautiful textures! Did you know the placenta weighs as much as the baby? You made this. You did this*! Kijk, die mooie vliezen. Mooie moederkoek*."

Yes, the Dutch word for placenta is 'mother cookie.' I've made my peace with terms like 'shame hair,' but 'mother cookie' was a bit much for me. I couldn't help thinking, "How could you invent such a term? Was there someone long ago who was hungry for a post-birth snack?" And – right on cue – the assistant asked, "Do you want to keep it?"

My wife and I both stared at her for ten full seconds, before I volunteered, "What?" The assistant explained, "*De moederkoek*. Some people like to keep it."

I wanted to know why. Are there really people who eat it? Is it a Dutch thing I don't know about? Is there a reason they call it 'Mother Cookie?' Maybe I don't want to know…

But my wife was looking at me over her shoulder, saying, "I don't know. Maybe we'll want it. We can plant a tree with it…"

As I watched my newborn being neglected, it occurred to me, "Let's not have this discussion now." Sometimes, just give the people what they want. I told the assistant, "Fine! Wrap it up. We'll take it."

For months afterward, if you'd come to our house and drop in for dinner, we'd be ready. We'd just have to look in the freezer for fish sticks, pizza, or if you ever wanted to try some 'Mother Cookie…'

DRUG PROBLEM

To this day, I have never managed to get myself antibiotics from a Dutch doctor. Although, we came close with my daughter one time. She was just a few years old, and she had an ear infection. We took her to our doctor, who told us, "I could prescribe antibiotics, but there is a worldwide crisis of Antibiotic-Resistant Microbes, and we all must do our part to use less. So – why don't you go home and get some rest?"

We protested, "No one is getting any rest! Our daughter is screaming all night in pain. Her mama is not sleeping. I'm not sleeping. We need some medicine." We were recommended some over-the-counter cream. It was at that point that we decided to try alternative medicine – the homeopathic doctor.

The new doctor started out with another typical Dutch doctor phrase: "What do you think is the problem?"

Like it's a medicine quiz.

"We think our daughter has an ear infection."

The doctor said, "You are right."

I half-expected to win a prize.

Then came the next question: "And what would you like me to do?"

I've heard this question more than once from Dutch doctors: "What do you think I should do?" It's not the best way to inspire confidence. My first reaction is always, "You're the doctor. Surprise me!"

But, looking at it another way, if a doctor asks, "What do you think I should do?", asking your opinion like you're some medical expert, it really is quite a compliment. I summoned up the manner of a doctor who'd been studying pediatrics for years, and I offered my advice. "I think I'd prescribe some medicine!"

The doctor quickly determined the root of the problem: an outer ear infection on her right side and an inner ear infection on the left side. We were given two prescriptions. Both had magically illegible scribbles, and we looked on in awe as the woman at the pharmacy actually seemed to understand what they meant. But we were taken aback when she delivered the medicine: chamomile oil and *zuurdruppels*. We thought this might be a mistake... But no, the woman explained that the oil was for the outer ear infection and the sour drops were for the inner ear. At home, we wrestled our poor child into position and administered the chamomile oil first. In with the cotton ball. And then the flip over and the sour, vinegar drops into the other ear.

It was then that it occurred to my wife: "We're mixing oil and vinegar in our daughter's head." And she wasn't getting healthier very quickly. ... But when she sneezed, the salad dressing tasted great.

The Netherlands is a country where you can get smart drugs over the counter, no problem. And you can get soft drugs over the counter, no problem. But if you want to get antibiotic medicine to heal your body, Dutch people say, "Get out of here, you sick, disgusting freak."

CHAPTER 21

DUTCH CHEAP

Quality vs Quantity

"How do you make copper wire? Put a copper penny in a room with a couple Dutchmen and watch them fight over it."

– My uncle (who is Jewish)

There's something charming about the stereotype that Dutch people are cheap. I think it's the fact that Dutch people seem to really believe it about themselves.

But are the Dutch really cheap? Or is it something else? Perhaps they're *zuinig*, which translates to somewhere between frugal & stingy. I realized the difference when I went to visit my Dutch mother-in-law. She lives right on the border of Limburg, and every time we show up, she serves us fruit pie *vlaai*. I dutifully balance the tiny plate on my knee, as she also offers me a cup of coffee on its saucer. And just when I've managed to balance all that, in comes the cookie tin. If anything, she's generous to a fault. Not exactly cheap.

It was when she offered the cookies that it happened. One time, after I chose a cookie, she slammed the cookie tin shut so quickly I almost lost a finger. And I thought: "Ha! I've got you!"

I said, teasingly, "So, it's just like they say in the books. You're cheap with those cookies!"

She asked, "What do you mean?"

I explained, "You closed the cookie tin so quickly. You must want to make sure I don't take more than one!"

And she said, "No, no… I close the cookie tin so that – when you want another cookie – the cookies, they are fresh."

And I thought, "Wow, that's a different way of looking at it… You actually care about quality."

In America, I don't remember having a cookie tin. Nor a cookie jar. What I remember is opening a pack of cookies and eating them until they were gone. I was eating for Quantity. Here in the Netherlands it's more about Quality. But I can imagine a lot of Americans take one look at the Dutch way and conclude: 'CHEAP.'

If anything, sometimes Dutch folks take the freshness concept a bit too far.

Me: "Where's my bread?"

My colleague: "What bread?"

Me: "The bread I bought and put here in the refrigerator."

My colleague: "There was no bread."

Me: "I bought it yesterday. A full loaf of bread."

My colleague: "Oh, the *old* bread! That was garbage, I threw it out."

You call this cheap? It's more wasteful than the Americans.

The Dutch are so fanatic about fresh bread that they make it nearly impossible to *buy* fresh bread. These days the supermarkets do their best, building in little mini-bakeries in every store on every street. But even then, the fresh stuff is frequently sold out. Of course, there's always a plentiful supply of 'factory bread,' which my wife refuses to buy. My wife abhors any preservatives with her food, including the preservative known as 'the refrigerator.'

When I first came to Nederland, there were so-called 'GFT' bio-waste bins in every home. Anything biodegradable would go in the bins, the city would pick them up, and no need to waste the bread. Amsterdam was composting before composting was cool! Unfortunately – in practice – everyone used the things approximately once. They got stinky. People started using them as normal garbage cans. Next came the friendly-reminder posters and leaflets: "Say, neighbors, metal isn't a vegetable!" And soon after that, the city apparently became fed up.

Nowadays, no more bio-waste bins. Yet the city of Amsterdam does a rather good job of reminding you how green they are by running things on 'green energy.' The trams, for example, run on electricity from turbines powered by the incinerator of all the food we throw away. So it's a bit green, I suppose.

I remember staying at a house in France for a week. The garbage can felt redundant. They had separate bins for paper, metal and four kinds of plastic. Plus, the house had its own compost bin. After all that, we didn't need a 'garbage can.' In the Netherlands – at least in Amsterdam – they do collect paper, glass and sometimes plastic. The bins quickly get clogged, resulting in mounds of recycling being dumped next to the bins, hence all over the street. Better to burn it, apparently. Gotta keep them trams running.

If you want a new understanding of the word *zuinig*, look no further than the favorite candy of the Netherlands: *drop*. I assume the reason it's called drop is because it's the flavor I usually drop on the floor at the movies. I hold it up to the screen, and if the light doesn't shine through: drop. It's black licorice. The least favorite flavor in most parts of the world is the most popular here. And there are so many different varieties of this odd flavor: hard, soft, sweet, salty. It's the salty candy I really can't understand. There are some types of drop I would describe as 'Industrial Accident Flavor.'

My wife constantly tries to convert me. She thinks someday I'll 'come to my senses' and realize *drop is lekker*. We'll be driving on a road trip, and she'll say, "Want something tasty?" Then she plops it in my mouth, and my senses are so assaulted, I almost steer us off the road into a ball of flame. My reaction is partly because of shock, and partly because – after tasting black licorice – my body shuts down and wants to stop tasting anything ever again.

I couldn't understand why Dutch people love *drop* so much. I looked at the ingredients: sugar. Anise flavor. And gelatin. But what is gelatin? I did a corporate show for the makers of gelatin. And according to their annual report, it's: cow hooves; cow bones; cow teeth; plus, a new innovation called 'Fallen animals.'

I had to ask, "I'm sorry: What are fallen animals?" It turns out they're the ones that are normally too sick to eat. It used to be that when they'd fall over and die, you'd have to throw them out with the bread. But now – thanks to a new industrial process – when they drop, the Dutch make *drop*. And that is *zuinig*.

CHAPTER 22
DUTCH URBAN
Tiny Big City

'Wie parkeert, betaalt.'

– Cition ad campaign

Nederland is a densely-populated country, but only in the urban areas. The amount of construction and urban planning that most cities dedicate to urban sprawl – the Netherlands spends on keeping cities small. Small and well-ordered. Yes, Nederland loves freedom – as long as you know your place. There's a place for the bikes, a place for pedestrians, a place for the cars, a place for the trams. And don't forget the boats! The Dutch spend so much money on building and rebuilding their streets, it can seem strange to some people. I once met a man from the Balkans, who said, "Nederland, if you want to spend some money fixing the streets, come to Serbia. Here, I think you're done."

But the Dutch are never done! Indeed, the Dutch term for 'Road Closed' is '*de straat is open,*' literally 'the street is open.' Clearly, they're thinking from the street's perspective, and sometimes a street just needs to breathe. Sometimes a street will be perfect for two weeks, and then it will be ripped up again for no apparent reason.

Dutch football guru Johan Cruyff once famously said, "Every disadvantage has its advantage." Perhaps Cryuff served as an adviser for Dutch road construction: "A street is only truly open when it is closed for traffic." Dutch people like ripping up the streets so much I think sometimes they do it just for fun. Or perhaps it's just to make work for people. The people I call the Brick Flippers. I've watched as they pull the bricks up from one side of the road and replace them on the other side. This is the code of the Brick Flippers: "Some bricks have been face-down for two weeks! We must flip them to the other side. We have to be fair to both sides of the brick."

In Chicago, where I grew up, the streets would only get fixed if it was an election year. There were so many potholes in Chicago we had a saying: 'You can always tell which drivers are drunk – they're the ones *not* swerving.' In Amsterdam, you don't need a car. Living in most Dutch cities is like living in Manhattan: who can afford the parking? In Amsterdam – if you do have a car – it had better be a Share Car. My father in-law had a car. We told him: "Do you have a spare set of keys? Now it's a Share Car."

We joined my father in-law in a game called 'How many times over can you pay to park?' The game started when – together – we bought a new car, which at that time involved a trip to the Cition Parking Company. Until we could switch our monthly parking permit to the new license plate, we'd have to pay an hourly rate to park, just like everyone else. In addition to the monthly permit, I was paying now with my phone app … But so was my father in-law.

Number of times we were paying for the car now: three.

You may know Cition Parking Services from their citywide ad campaign, '*Wie parkeert, betaalt*.' 'If you park, you pay.' Their job is to collect revenue for the city. But apparently business is so good they actually have enough money left over for an outdoor advertising campaign. I happen to know how much these outdoor 'ad routes' cost. It's thousands of euros a week! And this was just to share their revelation that, "Hey wow! Parking costs money."

Next, my app alerted me I was not allowed to change license plates. So, in fact I'd been paying to park our old car, which was now somewhere in Zeeland. Well, at least my father in-law's parking app was still paying the hourly rate. BUT it seems parking apps only work if you've typed in the correct license number, and he hadn't. By the time we realized the error, we had accrued three parking fines. We noticed a jolly little conference of parking agents partying around our car, abuzz with chatter about how many parking tickets they could put on the windshield before the schlemiel of an owner would notice. I joined my father-in-law in running over to the parking party to protest: "We're already paying three times over!" Oh, how they laughed.

In the end, we had to console ourselves that we were funding the next round of anti-sprawl infrastructure. That, or a new pointless ad campaign.

CHAPTER 23

DUTCH STANDARDS
Whose Quirks Are Worse

'Metric System Thriving in America's Inner Cities ...from kilos of cocaine to cc's of heroin to the Glock 9mm, inner-city youths possess a firmer grasp of the metric system than their peers in suburban and rural areas.'

– The Onion.com

Growing up in the United States, I was taught that 'American exceptionalism' was a good thing. But as soon as I learned the Metric system, I realized 'American exceptionalism' is frequently idiotic. How many NASA orbiters will we have to lose before we stop insisting on measuring distances based on the length of King Henry I's foot?

Then again, there are certain Dutch standards of measurement that are equally ridiculous. Being an expat means you get to pick and choose the best of both worlds – and reject the worst. Yes, it's time to play Ranking the Standards!

MEASURING

Start with the Metric system. The official one-meter measure is kept on display in the halls of science in Paris. So Dan Brown can write a mystery novel about it someday. That can only mean that – somewhere, the American system is keeping the foot of King Henry I, from 1100 AD. Of course, the official foot is not on display. Because it's shameful and weird. Score one point for the Dutch.

USA 0 – NED 1

COUNTING

Now that we're counting, let's admit the Dutch standard of counting is backward. Literally. The Dutch still say 24 as "four-and-twenty" – which was only ever practical when stuffing a pie with blackbirds. When Dutch people try to give you their phone numbers, it quickly gets ridiculous:

"06..."

I write down *06*.

"4 and fifty."

I write down *45*. And then I ERASE, as I realize it's *54*.

"6 and thirty."

I write down *63*. ERASE! Sorry: *36*.

"7..."

That's easy: *7*.

"3..." I write down *3*.

"...times zero."

ERASE!

Hopeless. Point USA.

USA 1 – NED 1

SCHEDULING

The American standard of giving the date is Month/Day/Year. That's like saying Winter/Summer/Spring.

Point Nederland.

USA 1 – NED 2

FLOOR COUNT

Most buildings count their floors from the good old number 1. But Dutch buildings start with the ground floor as 'Floor Zero.' For Americans, this is way too close to the term 'Ground Zero.' To make things even more confusing, a Dutch term for *floor* is *verdieping. Verdieping* means 'going deeper' – while you're actually going higher. No wonder MC Escher was Dutch.

Point USA.

USA 2 – NED 2

TEMPERATURE

The Fahrenheit scale makes it hard to convey how cold Chicago winters can be. If you say, "below zero," Dutch people will think, 'below freezing.' And I'll have to explain, "No, freezing is at 32 degrees Fahrenheit. Chicago is 32 degrees below freezing and then *more* degrees below *that.*" And then they're lost. Advantage Celsius.

Sometimes I notice Celsius is not quite as accurate when the weather gets warmer. 15C means '*maybe* bring a coat.' But in Chicago 60F means *definitely* bring a coat. Then again, in the Netherlands, you quickly learn to bring a coat even if the forecast is 20C. And – whatever you think of the Fahrenheit scale – you've got to give the Dutch credit for hosting Mr. Fahrenheit when he invented it.

Point Nederland.

USA 2 – NED 3

FAREWELLS

The Dutch say: "*Doei*!" The Yanks say, "Bye-bye." Both are equally silly, really. The Yanks say, "See you," whereas the Dutch say, "*Tot ziens,*" or "*Tot kijk,*" or "*Tot zo,*" or "*Tot later,*" or any number of options – which only increase the likelihood of me getting it wrong. I normally say, "Tot (mumble mumble)," so Dutch people can fill in the right one themselves. Then there's the Dutch formal farewell, "*De groeten.*" This translates to 'the greetings,' which is just backwards.

Point USA.

USA 3 – NED 3

PHOTOGRAPHY

When Dutch people aim a camera phone at you, they don't '*take* a picture,' they '*make* a picture.' The Dutch way makes more sense. When Americans say, "I want to *take* a picture," I always think *Airplane*, when the reporter says, "Let's take some pictures," and they steal the photos from the walls.

Point Nederland.

USA 3 – NED 4

TELLING TIME

In Britain 'half-ten' is 10:30. In Nederland 'half-ten' is 9:30. The Dutch are living in the future. The Americans say, "half PAST ten," which is on the side of the Brits. The Dutch think in terms of 'halfway to ten,' which is more forward-thinking. Then again, when I'm rushing for a train, the Dutch will hit me with bizarre phrases like '*tien over half negen,*' which means 'ten, minus 30, plus ten.' By the time I've figured that out, the train doors have closed in my face.

Minus one point Nederland.

USA 3 – NED 3

TERMINOLOGY

When Dutch folks want a cola, they order a 'cola.' Try that in the US:

"I'd like a cola."

"A *cola*? You mean like Coca-Cola?"

"Yes."

"We don't have Coca-Cola."

"What do you have?"

"Pepsi."

"Which is a...?"

"Cola."

"Which is why I ordered a *cola*."

Point Nederland.

USA 3 – NED 4

Nederland is the winner!

Why stop here? There are plenty more examples. I'll get to those in the quiz. But as of now it's the Netherlands with more common-sense standards than the Yanks or the Brits. You may not like these results and want to pound your fist in rage. But just know your pound is not as effective as a kilo.

CHAPTER 24

DUTCH CHEERLEADER
You Need a Wing Man

'Dutch Anti-Nationalist Nationalism'

– Kesic & Duyvendak, *The Paradox of Dutch National Identity*

Sometimes I think back to that seminar on 'Dutch Identity: Who Are We?' There was a speaker who highlighted two USPs of Dutch identity: being independent-minded; but also being non-hierarchical. Hence, everyone wants to be their own boss, but no one wants to be on top. He showed a study concluding that Nederland is the least chauvinistic country in Europe. In essence – if the Dutch do have a national identity – then they don't feel comfortable acknowledging it. Dutch folks are Old Money: "Yes we're filthy rich, but we don't like to talk about it."

If I could go back to that panel, there are a few things I'd like to say: "I took the citizenship course, and I recommend it. For Dutch people too! For example, not enough Dutch people know about *Het Plakkaat van Verlatinghe* – the Dutch Declaration of Independence. Independence from the Spanish king in 1581. There are phrases in the 1776 Declaration of Independence that Thomas Jefferson lifted straight from the Dutch version. When it comes to Freedom, it's Netherlands First, America Second."

"It's all there in black & white & orange: the Netherlands is the world's first modern republic. You had the world's first multinational company, the first stock exchange, the first multi-ethnic colony in the New World and the inspiration for the American Dream. Indeed – from dikes breaking to oil spilling to global warming – Dutch people have answers to a lot of the world's problems. The problem is the rest of the world has never heard about them. Because Dutch people are allergic to taking credit."

Nederland, take some credit! I get it, you're Dutch: being proud is not in your DNA. That's why you need a cheerleader. You need me. I'm Dutch enough to be proud of the Dutch, and American enough to not care how loud I am about it.

CHAPTER 25

THE DUTCH TOUCH
An Ode to Dutch Stuff

The Netherlands. You may know us from *Pulp Fiction, Ocean's Twelve,* and that scene from the Spider-Man movie that was clearly not filmed in the Netherlands.

But there are also Dutch influences all over the world, many of which you might not have noticed. A lot of them are just hiding in plain sight. If only we had someone to list a lot of them, preferably in rhyme. Here we go: An Ode to Dutch Stuff.

The artwork hanging on your wall.
The long-life light bulb in your hall.

Carrots that are orange – wow, who knew?
And WiFi – yes that's Dutch too.

The microscope. The telescope.
For some reason the name of a game of jump rope.

The book of maps known as the *atlas.*
The inventor of the word *podcast.*

Thermometers that use mercury.
The origin of the dollar currency.

The LED on your TV screen.
Manhattan, the cheapest real estate deal we've ever seen.

Half the place names in New York City.
The word *shoe* – the word *cookie.*

André Kuipers – the bald guy in space.
Yankee – from the Dutch names Jan & Kees.

Ketel One & the origin of Brandy.
Drop – the world's most disgusting candy.

The ones who made the first CDs.
And that scene from *Pulp Fiction:* 'Royale with Cheese.'

The first pump trucks for fires that were fighted.
The eye chart to find out if you're near-sighted.

The first operational submarine.
Senseo – the crappy coffee machine.

Bugaboo, Van Moof – with frames that are big.
WeTransfer – like You Send It, but free to 2 GB.

Senz the umbrella with wind-proof design.
Albertsons – the sons of Albert Heijn.

Lady Melisandra on *Game of Thrones.*
(And Daario, slipping Khalisi the bone.)

Pendulum clocks for keeping the time.
The ICC Court for International Crime.

Miffy the bunny, so cute you could eat.
And yes, even Zwarte Piet.

DJ Tiesto, Mata Hari.
The world's first speeding camera (sorry).

The ones who discovered New Zealand.
The inspiration for James Bond.

Basic Instinct, Robocop, Speed.
Capitalism: an economic model based on greed.

Philips, Shell, KLM.
Akzo Nobel, DSM.

Unilever, Heineken.
Anne Frank and Van Halen.

The origin of the Olympic Torch.
Hutspot a dish that looks like '*Blortsch.*'

Tony Chocolonely – guaranteed slave-free.
Keeping Manhattan safe from the sea.

People who are statistically the world's most tall.
Food – and women – served out of a wall.

The tulip fields the tourists trample.
The bad guy from *The Fugitive* – "you switched the samples!"

Doutzen Kroes, Skater Sven Kramer.
The passenger who took out the Underwear Bomber.

Blade Runner Baddie – Rutger Hauer.
Crappy music by Frans Bauer.

Dubai Islands in the shape of a palm.
TOMTOM, former colony Suriname.

MC Escher, Hieronymus Bosch.
Rembrandt, Vincent van Gogh.

The one-time owners of Ben & Jerry's.
Legal gay marriage for when Harry met Larry.

Erasmus, Spinoza, René Descartes.
And Michael van Gerwen – world champion, Darts.

The first-ever Fair-Trade coffee.
The 'Netherlands Second' video, starring me.

The nr. 2 Agri-Exporter on the planet.
And if your river overflows, they will dam it.

...In total, they've offered the world so much.
But if you take credit, you're not truly Dutch.

PART TWO

THE QUIZ

SECTION ONE
THE ACTUAL QUIZ

CHAPTER 1
INBURGERINGS EXAM
Sample question

As promised, there will be a quiz. Let's start out with some questions from the actual exam. The first few levels of the quiz are questions from the 'Nationale Inburgering Test' at NTR.nl – the closest I could find to the questions I had in my course. [*Translation via Google / Shapiro*]

To pass the online exam you need 5.5 out of 10. It sounds easy, but there's one group of people who traditionally have a hard time: Dutch people.

The online exam even gives you some examples of how some famous Dutch people have scored.

Jacques d'Ancona (TV journalist) 4.7
Howard Komproe (comedian) 4.6
Victoria Koblenko (soap actress) 4.0

Note: none of them achieved 5.5.

Now is your chance to prove you're more Dutch than famous Dutch people!

One year, the Dutch Assimilation Test appeared on TV. The winners were Chinese food delivery guys. In any given classroom full of people taking this exam, there's a real sense of solidarity as everyone looks around and shrugs, "I have no idea."

SAMPLE QUESTION

What or who is commemorated on the 4th of May?

B All war victims

C The beginning of World War II

D The end of World War II

ANSWER = A

As 5 May is Liberation Day, 4 May is Memorial Day. Who exactly is being memorialized? That part has been subject to change. One thing that doesn't change: at 8 P.M., shut up for two minutes.

The more practical question would be:
HOW do the Dutch commemorate war victims on the 4th of May?
Answer: With two minutes of silence at 8 P.M.

A friend of mine arrived in the Netherlands in the month of April and – by the time 4 May rolled around – he had no idea about the two-minute silence. He was just happy he could navigate the laundromat. There he was, putting coins into the laundromat dryer and successfully turning it on. But at 8 P.M., an older woman came up. She opened the door and turned the dryer off. My friend – having just lost his money – yelled at the woman in his best Dutch. But she frantically gestured at him to be quiet. What followed was two minutes of the worst game of charades ever, which abruptly ended at 8:02, when she walked away. And he had no idea why. This is how NOT to commemorate the 4th of May.

CHAPTER 2

ESSENTIAL KNOWLEDGE

Many of these questions have been criticized as too subjective. But I say: that's what makes them perfect! A simple analysis of each question reveals more about the Dutch mentality than the exam ever intended.

QUESTION 1

How did nutmeg first arrive in the Netherlands?

A From our colony in the Antilles

B From our colony Indonesia

C From our colony Suriname

ANSWER = B

But more important is that you know the Netherlands had COLONIES.

QUESTION 2

Where is the tulip bulb industry the biggest?

A In Flevoland

B In Noord-Holland

C In Zuid-Holland

ANSWER = B

Hopefully, if you're taking this test you're no longer picking tulip bulbs.

QUESTION 3

Your colleague from work is getting married. You are not invited to the wedding, but you want to do something nice. What do you do?

A You give a gift, for example something for the kitchen
B You give an envelope with money
C You send a card

ANSWER = C

I've asked this question to hundreds of Dutch people. When I ask why, the answer is invariably, "Because it's cheap."

CHAPTER 3

EVERY QUESTION TELLS A STORY

It's not about answering the questions. The real lesson is the logic *behind* the questions.

QUESTION 1

You are sitting with a colleague at a terrace. At the table next to you there are two men kissing and caressing each other. You are bothered by this. What do you do?

A You remain seated and act as if you are not offended
B You tell the men that they should go sit somewhere else
C You say loudly to your colleague what you think about homosexuality

ANSWER = A

My favorite part of this question is the assumption: 'You are bothered by this.' Personally, I would not be bothered by this. But to answer the question correctly, you have to pretend to be someone who IS bothered by this, pretending NOT to be bothered by this.

Incidentally, most Dutch people I've met *would* say something. It's a terrace. And the men are not just kissing, they're 'kissing and caressing.' I would not be surprised to hear someone say, *"Doe normaal!"*

QUESTION 2

The neighbors on your street have placed a wooden stork in their garden. They've just had a baby. You are friendly with the neighbors and they always greet you. What should you do first?

A Put a greeting card in their postbox

B Visit your neighbors to see the baby
C Wait a few days and then visit the baby

ANSWER = A

In other words: you never drop in on your neighbors unannounced. When Dutch people say, "You must come over sometime..." what they *mean* is you should pull out an agenda and say, "How about the third Thursday next month?"

These are the same people who have their front windows at street level with the curtains wide open, so you can look in and see everything they're doing. But if you ring the doorbell without an appointment, they'll close the curtains and hide in the corner like, "We're not here!"

QUESTION 3

You smell gas in your rental apartment. What should you do?
A Open all the windows and doors and call the utility company
B Close all the windows and doors and call an accredited installation company
C Close the gas valve and call the local housing department

ANSWER = A

There are some very useful tips here, but they're not in the same answer.
If you open all the windows. You're rather safe.
If you also shut off the gas valve, you are very safe.
But – according to the exam – you're not Dutch.

CHAPTER 4
RIGHT ANSWER VS TRUE ANSWER

It is important to know how the Dutch see themselves. It is also important to know the truth.

QUESTION 1

How did the Dutch start the tradition of lighting fireworks on New Year's?

A To chase evil spirits away

B To make New Year's Eve extra festive

C Because the Chinese did it. We took it over

RIGHT ANSWER = A

Historically, the Dutch chased away evil spirits by gathering together to make loud noises. (Again, you can see why this is essential knowledge.)

TRUE ANSWER = B

Whatever the historical background, the fact is that New Year's Eve in the Netherlands is an enormous party. My first New Year's Eve in the Netherlands was in the late '90s on Leidseplein. Coming from America, we hear 'fireworks,' and we think of the 4th of July, with Independence Day fireworks coordinated by the local governments. The displays start with fireworks going off one by one, then they get a little faster, and they end with a bunch of fireworks going off all in a row.

But in the Netherlands, after the countdown "5-4-3-2-1..." it's Shock and Awe. 360 degrees of bombs bursting in air. Everyone in every street is lighting their own private stash of fireworks. We even tried it one year. As a word of caution: when you want to launch a rocket, don't do what I did.

I'd watched my neighbors using a champagne bottle as a stand to launch their rockets, and I did the same – but I didn't think to fill mine with water. We lit the fuse, we stood well back, and then we watched as the wind tipped the bottle over as the rocket fired. The rocket took off horizontally – at about face-level – and exploded in the street a block away. We looked to see if anyone was hurt, but all we saw was a single bicyclist coming towards us with a very large frown. The way I remember it is slightly cartoonish. I could swear his bike was still smoking.

For years, there would be a small economic boom every December in the form of fireworks purchases. Even if the economy had slipped into recession, the Dutch had a habit of breaking new records in fireworks spending, time after time. What better way to celebrate a crisis? Take your investments and literally watch them go up in smoke.

QUESTION 2

If Dutch people come across other Dutch people in a foreign country, what do they do?

A They respect each other's privacy
B They think, "How nice" and invite them to dinner
C The question doesn't apply, as they always go on group vacations with other Dutch people

RIGHT ANSWER = B (This never happens.)

TRUE ANSWER = A

When they're abroad, most Dutch people I've seen avoid each other like Superman & Kryptonite.

My wife and I were on a boat tour in the US once, and we heard another family speaking Dutch to each other. My wife was so concerned that they might hear her speaking to me with a Dutch accent that she adopted a British accent tor two hours. No matter what, she wanted to avoid getting into that conversation:

"OH! Bent u ook Nederlandse!? Waar komen jullie vandaan? Wij komen uit Purmerend! Wat een leuke wolkenkrabbers, hoor!"

QUESTION 3

Dutch people go on vacation mostly

A In Nederland

B In France or Spain

C Elsewhere

RIGHT ANSWER = A 'We have Center Parcs for a reason!'

TRUE ANSWER = B

Summer in Nederland is like a flooding drill. Everyone pretends like the country is finally underwater, so they pack up everything they own and drive south.

I've been on summer vacation in France, and the road is always choked with Dutch cars. We were standing still in traffic on the road by Orléans, and it was nothing but yellow license plates. You couldn't swing a dead cat without hitting a Dutch camper trailer, aka 'caravan,' aka *sleurhut* (or 'Drag Hut').

Maybe that's why Dutch people take everything along when they go camping. We once saw a car that was too cool for a caravan; they'd just crammed everything into the back of their station wagon. The kids were playing their Nintendos with their faces pressed up against the windows. There was one poor girl with a sleeping bag on one side of her face, and a tent pole poking at her from above. And on the other side, there was something blue pressing up against her head, but we couldn't tell what it was. We pulled up a bit closer, and we saw it was a Senseo coffee machine, with the cylinder for their own coffee pads, "Because they might not have coffee in France."

That's the way Dutch folks go on holiday.

SECTION TWO
THE QUESTIONS THAT SHOULD BE ON THE ACTUAL QUIZ

(from *How to Be Dutch: The Quiz*)

CHAPTER 5
DUTCH IDENTITY

It can be difficult to understand the Dutch identity. Even Dutch people have a hard time figuring it out.

QUESTION 1
What is the name of this country?
A Holland
B Nederland
C The Netherlands

ANSWER = B (& C)

In the Dutch language, the name of the country is *Nederland*. In English it's *the Netherlands.* Oddly – of the 12 Dutch provinces – only two have *Holland* in the title. This may help explain the result of so many Dutch World Cup football teams. Yes, there are legions of orange-clad Dutch fans, but they yell, "Holland! Holland!" And when the ball goes to the player from, say, Friesland, a part of them must think, "I'm not from Holland." And they miss.

QUESTION 2

When Dutch people brag about their country, what examples do they use?

A Dutch brands

B Dutch water engineering

C Dutch sports & entertainment

ANSWER = NONE OF THE ABOVE

Trick question! Dutch people never brag about their country. At best, they humble-brag by saying America is first, and then politely asking to be second. So partial credit for C.

Internationally, yes the Dutch are quietly known for their masterful water engineering. But you don't see the Delta Works on Dutch t-shirts. Perhaps the term *Afsluitdijk* isn't catchy enough for bumper stickers. And what about the Maeslantkering? These gates that protect the Port of Rotterdam are an engineering marvel, each gate as large as the Eiffel Tower. But – unlike the Eiffel Tower – they don't appear on keychains, coffee mugs or refrigerator magnets. In Nederland, these items largely feature the noble cannabis leaf. Meaning, by default, the most popular form of Dutch water engineering is the bong.

As a footnote, Dutch bragging can sometimes appear as a result of Dutch people insulting other countries. A Dutch Olympic coach was once interviewed on American TV about the fact that his Dutch speed skating team had won more medals than any team in Olympic history. One would expect him to start talking about how proud he was. But instead, he started by insulting American athletes and, for some reason, American football. And then – when of course the interview turned into an argument – he ended up defending the Netherlands by listing successful Dutch brands: "When we'd sell our companies to the world, we'd all be billionaires! When we'd sell Shell, Unilever, Aegon… man, you're broke!"

So partial credit for A.

QUESTION 3

How many times does the Dutch national anthem reference other countries?

A 1

B 2

C 3

ANSWER = C

The Dutch *volkslied* is called *Het Wilhelmus*. We had to learn it in our citizenship class. It starts: '*Wilhelmus van Nassouwe, ben ik van Duitsen bloed.*' Literally translated: 'I'm William, founder of your country, and by the way I'm German.' Yes, German. (My instructor explained, "It doesn't really mean German." I asked, "Where is Nassouwe?" We looked it up on the map. It's in Germany.) And follow up question: Are there any other countries that start their national anthem by name checking a different nation? Most countries think of their anthem as a chance to to express their national pride. Not the Netherlands. The Dutch anthem is more like, "Hi, we're a country, but let's not talk about us. Germany is nice..."

In fact, the Dutch don't talk about themselves for the entire song. And then in the final line, just when the rest of the world is thinking, "Here comes their name..." Nope: it's Spain. '*Den koning van Hispanje heb ik altijd geëerd*' or 'My allegiance for all time has been to the King of Spain.' So Spain is the second country referenced. (My instructor explained, "This is not the end of the original text!" The original text was many stanzas, together forming a rallying cry for the Dutch revolution – against the Spanish. Without that part, the song basically ends with: 'We respect our oppressors! We may have Stockholm Syndrome.')

So far that's two countries mentioned, neither being Nederland. Can you imagine America starting off its national anthem: 'O say can you see – our British history? And Canada is our hat. And we just love that Mexico' –? And it's no wonder the Netherlands never actually wins the World Cup. Every time the men's team manage to reach the World Cup final, they start out by pledging allegiance to their opponents. Think about it: Germany 1974; Spain 2010. Coincidence?

The closest *Het Wilhelmus* comes to national pride is the line '*Een Prins van Oranje*,' or 'A prince from Orange.' Orange is a city in France. Hence a total of three other countries are referenced. And they're not just any three countries. As you can read in any history book, these are all countries that have invaded and occupied the Netherlands. Hence, the question: 'What kind of self-hating country has this text as a national anthem?'

This would be the American equivalent of starting the national anthem: 'O say can you see? Vietnam was a FAIL. And Iraq was a lie, but then no one went to jail. Everything we've done wrong, we have put it in this song. And no, we're not done, because the list is quite long...'

Nederland, you have a lovely country. Lovely culture. But you deserve a better national anthem.

CHAPTER 6
DUTCH BIKES

In the city of Amsterdam, the population is an estimated 900,000 people – and 1 million bikes. In the rest of the Netherlands, the proportion is roughly the same. We don't know how the bikes are repopulating, but clearly they've outnumbered the humans.

QUESTION 1

While biking, you see a group of tourists edging toward the bike path ahead of you. When should you ring your bell?

A Ring as early and as often as possible
B Dutch bikes don't have bells
C Wait until you are almost on top of them

ANSWER = C

Ringing one's bell more often than necessary is for tourists. And while it's true many Dutch bikes don't have bells, most of them do. Even broken down, old bikes will have their bells replaced before, say, their brakes. The most Dutch answer is to wait until the last moment and ring your bell frantically, perhaps yelling, "*Klootzak.*"

Dutch cyclists are very optimistic. As the weather gets warmer and tourists start to arrive, the cyclists continue at full speed, believing nothing will impede their progress. Dutch cyclists will ring their bells as if genuinely surprised that newcomers don't know the distinction between sidewalk and bike path. By waiting until the last possible moment to ring, Dutch bikes maximize the element of surprise for the tourists, who will jump out of the way in terror and yell, "WTF!?" This is a tradition for the Dutch as well as for tourists who need the exercise. It's called the 'Tring-Tring WTF' Diet.

QUESTION 2

When is it okay to judge people on the basis of color?

A Never

B When you're in the Netherlands

C When you see a group of bikes of the same color

ANSWER = C

While biking in the Netherlands, it is never okay to judge people on the basis of color. Unless they're riding a group of matching-colored bicycles. Then you can be sure they are tourists on rental bikes, who are way more dangerous than when they're on foot. They're possibly high, and they probably don't know how to bike. Just the other day, I was almost run over by a group of matching green bikes. They were all blithely biking through a red light, as if assuming 'green bikes mean green lights.'

QUESTION 3

When parking your bike in a row of bikes, you knock over someone else's bike. What should you do?

A Set the bike back upright

B Leave the bike on the ground

C Set the bike back upright and then knock over more bikes in the process

ANSWER = C

In the Netherlands, there are so many bikes it's hard to knock over just one. In Amsterdam, the city has been removing bike racks and replacing them with bike parking areas marked on the pavement. This strategy is designed to make life easier – not for you, but for bike thieves and for the city's bike removal teams. Either way, there is a cull of bicycle overpopulation.

When parking your bike in an area without a rack, it is likely you will knock over a series of bikes, who will fall like dominoes. It is also likely there will be witnesses. The witnesses may well be tourists, who may well be high on something and laughing hysterically. This is understandable, since what you've done is frankly hilarious. You might be tempted to ask them for help, which – given their sense of coordination – is unwise. Simply set your bike upright and as many other bikes as time will allow (according to one Dutch source, 'maximum 2 minutes'). And remember – any bikes falling outside of the white square on the pavement will be removed by the city. Don't worry. This is a natural process, known as bike euthanasia.

CHAPTER 7

DUTCH HOUSING

Compared to the United States, the Netherlands has a relatively small homeless problem. How they manage this feat is mystery, because it can be very difficult to find housing. Very.

QUESTION 1

What is the rationale behind Dutch staircases?

A To celebrate Dutch nautical history

B To be efficient with space

C To punish humanity

ANSWER = B & C

Dutch staircases are notorious for being bizarrely steep, twisted and inhumane – in other words, 'normal.' Some older Dutch houses feature staircases that seem to have been literally ripped out of old ships. Obviously, when floor space is limited, it's necessary to be efficient with space. But even in newer, more spacious housing, Dutch building codes still require steepness and a maximum number of twists and turns. It's no wonder the Dutch word for staircase is *trap* – as in 'something you fall into.'

QUESTION 2

What is the Dutch version of 'Full Bath?'

A Bathtub that is full

B An empty room with a showerhead

C A full bathroom, with bathtub / shower, toilet and sink

ANSWER = B

In Dutch housing, there is rarely a bathtub. More likely there is a showerhead in one corner, with not even the pretense of a shower curtain. Rather, there may be a squeegee, with which Dutch people can engage in their favorite pastime of moving water where they want it to go. The toilet will be located in a separate room, where the aromas of defecation can be more acutely concentrated.

QUESTION 3

Which are acceptable structures for Dutch housing?

A Squatted flat
B Abandoned shipping containers
C Abandoned office building
D Abandoned boat

ANSWER = EVERYTHING EXCEPT A

Dutch housing organizations are rewarded for their creativity with unclaimed structures, such as boats, offices and, yes, even stacks of shipping containers. But if you try to exercise this same creativity by squatting in an actual house, you will be treated like a terrorist.

CHAPTER 8

DUTCH SEX LIFE

Dutch culture treats sex as a natural part of life, which is healthy, really.

QUESTION 1

How can you best describe Dutch attitudes toward the Red Light District?

A "We don't go there"

B "Other countries have them too. What's so special about ours?"

C "We're proud of our adult-themed amusement park"

ANSWER = A & B

If you want to fit into most Dutch conversations, it's: "We don't think about it. We don't talk about it. And if you do talk about it, you're probably a tourist."

QUESTION 2

Which of the following is offered at a Dutch health and beauty shop?

A My First Vibrator

B Penis lollies

C Candy G-String

ANSWER = ALL OF THE ABOVE

In the Netherlands, you can pop in to buy some toothpaste and be confronted with the standard selection of a sex shop. Candy G-strings and edible undies can be found right next to the wide variety of lube and protection. And penis-shaped lollies have been known to pop up from time to time. And yes, Dutch health and beauty shops will offer vibrators. Specifically, the 'My First Vibrator' was a free gift with a subscription to *Viva* magazine. *Viva* features the 'Any Body' column, in which Dutch couples pose nude – with their heads cropped out. Are all Dutch folks exhibitionists? I don't know. But *Viva* never seems to have a shortage of nude volunteers.

QUESTION 3

What is the correct order for Dutch dating?

A Date, sex, phone call
B Sex, date, phone call
C Date, phone call, sex

ANSWER = B

Many cultures advocate a getting-to-know-you phase before engaging in sex. Example: "I've been dating someone for a few weeks. And I'm thinking it's time to invite him to bed." Dutch friends of mine find this idea ridiculous: "Why would you spend three weeks on a guy, if he might be bad in bed?"

In America, it's: "Take me to dinner, then maybe you can take me to bed." In Nederland, it's: "Take me to bed, then maybe we can go to dinner." ("But I'm only going to pay half.")

CHAPTER 9
DUTCH OFFICE CULTURE

The Dutch invented the microscope, WiFi and Capitalism. And some of the most convoluted decision-making the world has ever seen.

QUESTION 1

What is the best way to present your idea to a Dutch business meeting?

A "I have a great idea"

B "I like your idea, but my idea is better"

C "Your idea is stupid"

ANSWER = C

Option A is not advisable, as – again – Dutch culture seems to be allergic to anything resembling '*opscheppen*' or *bragging*. That is when a built-in bullshit detector will kick in and cut you off at the knees. Option B is acceptable, but it goes against the Dutch belief in equality, and they may have to cut you down to size. Saying, "Your idea is stupid" is the most uniquely Dutch response.

As an experiment, you can try Option A "I have a great idea" – and watch as the response is Option C: "Your idea is stupid. The place you come from is stupid. And your beard looks like you have pubic hair on your face." (actual quote)

QUESTION 2

How can you tell who's in charge of a Dutch meeting?

A The one who's most dominant

B The one with the most expensive suit

C The one who arrives by bike

ANSWER = C

Most countries are rather hierarchical: the boss says it; you do it. Not in Nederland. The boss may well arrive by bike. Like Dutch topography, Dutch management culture is flat as a *pannenkoek*. The Netherlands is a river delta, and this country is so flat that even a city called 'Seven Mountains' (*Zevenbergen*) is one meter under sea level. That's perhaps the reason why Dutch people are so tall. The short ones drowned.

A In general, Dutch bosses have a reputation for being non-hierarchical and down to earth. Even the Dutch prime minister is known for biking to work and cleaning up his own spilled coffee. I was once walking into a café in Den Haag, when I saw Prime Minister Mark Rutte walking out and putting his suit coat on. I saw that his collar was messed up, so I pointed it out to him. And I ended up fixing his collar for him. It only occurred to me later that – in AmericI would have been shot.

QUESTION 3

How many vacation days are standard in the Netherlands?

A Two weeks

B Four weeks

C Six weeks – plus vacation pay – but that's my final offer

ANSWER = C

In America, you're lucky to get two weeks off in a row. In the Netherlands, if your summer break is less than three weeks, people think there's something wrong with you. I remember my first job in the Netherlands, when I was granted three whole weeks of vacation time. I refused to use them. I didn't want my boss to think I was lazy. She told me, "I don't think you're lazy; I think you're *crazy*."

And then my boss told me about vacation pay. Yes, they were also giving me 8% of my annual salary to spend on my vacation. They not only wanted to me out of the office – they were bribing me to stay away! It took some getting used to – for about 5 minutes. It was classic case of Dutch Culture Shock Therapy: it felt weird and wrong... until I realized it was actually much better than what I was used to. These days, when I go back to visit the US, I'm reminded of the Top 3 Reasons I don't move back to the US: Transportation, Education – and No Vacation.

CHAPTER 10

DUTCH FASHION

If you encounter women wearing skirts over their jeans or men wearing orange trousers, it must be the Netherlands. Men will also wear trousers the color of mustard or ketchup. This is to hide stains.

QUESTION 1

What kinds of undershirt are allowed for men?

A Tight, white crewneck T-shirt
B White V-neck T-shirt
C A T-shirt showing Mr. Happy with an enormous penis

ANSWER = A

As for the Mr. Happy T-shirt, that will be worn onstage by many a Dutch comedian, to be as distracting as possible.

V-neck T-shirts are apparently out of style in the Netherlands, based on the absolute lack of demand. While some cultures encourage men to loosen their collars and reveal a bit of flesh – or maybe chest hair – the Dutch are different. In a Dutch office, if men ever loosen their collars, it's to reveal the pristine curve of their white undershirt, as if to say, "Relax, everyone! No pheromones escaping here!"

Even the Mormons – who are required to wear special undergarments at all times – will take pains to hide their underwear from view when possible. But, like the Mormons, Dutch men obey the white T-shirt rule religiously, sending a clear message to rest of the world: I probably have tightie-whitie underpants as well.

As they say online, 'a well-tailored suit is to a woman as lingerie is to a man.' If that's true, then the effect of a tight, white undershirt is less 'Victoria's Secret' and more like 'Victoria's full-length bathing costume.'

QUESTION 2

What constitutes normal dress?

A Dressing as a huge orange lion

B Dressing as an overtly racist stereotype

C Dressing with at least one item of clothing from *Hema*

ANSWER = ALL OF THE ABOVE

If there are Dutch people with no *Hema* in their wardrobe, I haven't met them. As for the rest, normal dress is dictated by '*doe normaal*,' which depends on the calendar. If it's King's Day, or if the Dutch national team is playing in an international tournament like the World Cup, then you may want to join in wearing orange – or go dressed as an orange lion.

As to racist stereotypes, yes there is a time of year for that. No, not Sinterklaas: Carnival. For Carnival, aka *Mardi Gras*, school children will feel left out if they do not come to school in costume. In the southern provinces, the adults will join in, and apparently the theme is 'No taste, no problem.' Many a Dutch party store will be happy to sell you an unabashedly racist costume, such as 'Chinaman,' 'African Hottentot,' and – for the culturally sensitive – 'Hip Hottentot' with blond afro instead of black.

QUESTION 3

Dutch women's hairstyles are frequently shorter than those of Dutch men. Why is this?

A To look like men

B To avoid spending money on excess hair products

C To protest the monarchy

ANSWER = NONE OF THE ABOVE

It's so they can more easily grab their 'wet rag' *watjes* men by the hair and show them who wears the trousers in the house.

CHAPTER 11

DUTCH EDUCATION

Today's Dutch schools focus on teaching students the basics: Critical thinking; Problem solving; and Communication skills. Or at least learning how to operate machines that do that for you.

QUESTION 1

At what age do Dutch kids grow up?

A 11

B 18

C They never grow up

ANSWER = A

I was reading one of those articles about how Dutch kids are the happiest in the world. Every so often someone does a survey and finds that – instead of pushing kids to perform well on tests – Dutch schools let kids be kids. It makes sense. What do you know? Kids are happier without homework! I've also noticed this trend with my own kids – up to a point. That point is called 11 years of age.

You know the American ritual called 'Going to College?' It's the biggest decision of your life up to that point, and it normally takes place at age 17. But Dutch kids have to make that kind of decision around age 11, when they pick their high school. And it's not just about which school; it's about which level of school and the right educational track for the career you want. Do you want to make things with your hands? Or do you want to work in management? Do you want to focus on academia and research? "You're 11, time to make up your mind and move on with your life!"

Yes, the Dutch school system lets kids be kids. Until it yanks them by the hair, smacks them in the face, and says, "Get a job!"

QUESTION 2

At what age do Dutch children learn about slavery?

A Primary school
B Junior High school
C High school
D By accident

ANSWER = D

If Dutch children learn about the Dutch slave trade, it's largely by accident. Maybe it's because Dutch history books are modest, and they don't like to brag. So they don't take too much credit for anything, even if it's something as notable as the Atlantic Slave Trade, history's largest forced intercontinental migration. Dutch history books are more comfortable covering slavery in terms of who *bought* the slaves, not who sold them.

Luckily, there's the Dutch national institute for Slavery, NiNsee, whose job is to provide education and awareness about this vital chapter in Dutch history. At least that was the case until 2011, when the Dutch government completely cut their funding. *Doei!*

QUESTION 3

When hiring an intern from a Dutch school, which level of education provides the best result?

A University
B HBO
C MBO

ANSWER = C

As it has been explained to me by employers; yes, there's always entry-level work that needs to be done. And yes, you should hire interns from schools! It's a win / win situation. But only if you pick the right educational level.

- If you want an intern to write a thesis on why the entry-level work is not good enough, then hire a university kid.
- If you want an intern to offer advice on how you should restructure your business model, then hire an HBO kid.
- If you want someone to do the work, then go MBO.

CHAPTER 12
DUTCH HOLIDAYS

If you can make the effort to understand the logic behind Dutch holidays, then you will understand more than most Dutch people.

QUESTION 1

Which of the following is NOT a national holiday?

A New Year's Day
B King's Day
C Liberation Day
D Ascension Day
E Second Ascension Day
F Pentecost
G Boxing Day

ANSWER = E

New Year's Day was made a holiday for practical reasons, mostly because everyone was out the night before, suffering fireworks-related injuries. King's Day used to be Queen's Day, because it was the Queen's mother's birthday, we think (but we're not sure due to the heavy drinking).

Liberation Day is nice, but most people are still hung over from King's Day. And Boxing Day is a holiday when you visit your in-laws and end up fighting with them because they weren't good enough to spend Christmas Day with.

The rest of the holidays are of course based on the Christian calendar, even though a majority of modern Dutch people describe themselves as 'non-religious.' Ascension Day (*Hemelvaart*) and Pentecost (*Pinksteren*) are official holidays, and some years you will get a second day off for both. If you want to be entertained, ask why the shops are closed and watch as no two people give the same answer: "It's from the Bible... you know, the time Jesus took a three-day weekend -?"

QUESTION 2

Which is a common way to celebrate King's Day?

A Wearing orange and indulging in substance abuse
B Wearing orange and selling a bunch of your old crap
C Wearing orange and making your kids sing and dance for money
D Not wearing orange and celebrating the Dutch Republic

ANSWER = EVERYTHING EXCEPT D

On King's Day, the Dutch dress in orange to honor the royal House of Orange, which goes all the way back to Willem van Oranje in the 1500s. Founding father Willem van Oranje led the revolution to overthrow the Spanish monarchy. So, do the Dutch celebrate their independence on Dutch independence day? No, that's in July, and everyone is on vacation – many of them in Spain. Instead, Dutch independence is celebrated on the birthday of the current Dutch monarch, which makes no sense at all.

On King's Day, it is quite common to join the orange-clad crowd in the nearest city center and abuse the substance of your choice. Since King's Day is also the beginning of the official tourist season, be sure to tell any arriving tourists, "Yes, we do this every day." I know someone who happened to arrive in the Netherlands at the end of April, and her first experience with Dutch culture was King's Day in Amsterdam. She was like, "Is every day going to be like this? I guess it's true what they say about this place!"

But a truly Dutch way to celebrate King's Day is to set up a mini street stand and get rid of old crap from your closet. Especially since it's a tiny country – and storage space in the average Dutch home is highly valued – the act of creating new storage space can feel a lot like Christmas.

There's even a King's Day for kids. But fair warning: Dutch kids may rope you into creating elaborate games of skill, involving cans and balls and lots of rope. Or they'll give quirky high-concept performances. I once encountered a group of girls around the age of ten. Their parents were asking 50 cents to look inside a tent labeled 'Peep show!' This seemed all kinds of wrong. But I paid my 50 cents, I stuck my head in the tent, and there was the group of girls, dressed as baby chickens saying, "Peep! Peep! Peep!" In the Netherlands, even the kids are politically incorrect.

QUESTION 3

On which occasion is it more important to give gifts to children?

A 5th of December for Sinterklaas

B 25th of December for Christmas

C Both

ANSWER = A

Yes, Sinterklaas still wins. But Christmas is gaining in popularity. Some Dutch purists lament that Sinterklaas should be for toys, and Christmas should be for Jesus. Even though more and more 7-year-olds are saying, "How am I supposed to believe in Jesus if he doesn't bring me toys?"

CHAPTER 13
ZWARTE PIET

In the Netherlands, every November heralds the arrival of Sinterklaas with his white horse and his army of *negers*. As Dutch people will explain, the word *neger* is not offensive, because it simply means 'Black person.'

QUESTION 1

Which of the following did NOT appear on Twitter in relation to criticism of Zwarte Piet?

A 'You're only here because you're Black'
B 'My ancestors indeed forced your ancestors onto the boats. Those were the days. Now your sort has too much freedom'
C 'F** the f*** off if you think Zwarte Piet is racist… you're retards'
D 'F*** off you black monkeys. Next you'll want to close all the zoos because you're afraid you might meet an ancestor'
E '#ZwartePietMatters'

ANSWER = A

That quote was attributed to Dutch football legend Johan Cruyff, as he was talking to Edgar Davids during a board meeting for Amsterdam Ajax. But he could get away with it, because they thought he was Jesus. RIP.

The other quotes are all real, and the overall behavior of the Zwarte Piet defenders has become so awful that they've helped force right-wing politicians like Prime Minister Rutte to admit Zwarte Piet needs to change.

And then there are politicians like Geert Wilders, who tweeted #ZwartePietMatters, during the Dutch #BlackLivesMatter protests. While most of the world was wondering, 'Who could possibly be more self-serving and racist than Donald Trump?' Wilders was like: "HOLD MY BEER."

Geert Wilders grew up with dark hair from his Indonesian background. But as an adult he started dying his hair – to hide his dark roots. And now that he dyes his hair blond, he apparently wants to continue painting his face black. So – whether he knows it or not – Wilders is actually Post-Racial. He's a brown man pretending to be a white man pretending to be a Black man.

QUESTION 2

Which alternative Zwarte Piet character has NOT been tried?

A Rainbow Piet
B *Kaas* Piet (Cheese Piet)
C *Stroopwafel* Piet (Waffle Cookie Piet)
D Gold Piet
E Soot & Beard Piet

ANSWER = E

Dutch people pride themselves on their common-sense, pragmatic approach to problem-solving. So, instead of actually making Zwarte Piet look like someone who came down a chimney, they've tried every other option imaginable. Rainbow Piet was laughed off the parade route in the 1990s. Cheese Pete looks like he has jaundice, and Waffle Cookie Piet looks like he has a flesh-eating virus. Soot-face Pete, or *Roet* Piet, is already being phased into Amsterdam's annual parade. Understandably, those dressing as Zwarte Piet are concerned that soot won't provide enough of a disguise for the little ones.

The idea of soot plus a beard – like Sinterklaas wears – has apparently not occurred to anyone.

QUESTION 3

Which cookies are currently sold in the Netherlands?

A *Neger Zoenen*

B *Choco Zoenen*

C *Negen Zoete*

ANSWER = C

For years, Dutch confectioner Buys produced chocolate-covered marshmallow cookies called *Neger Zoenen*. (*Zoenen* means kisses.) (*Neger* you can guess.) At some point, an anti-discrimination group politely asked, "Wouldn't you be able to sell more of your product without pointlessly insulting an entire color of people?" And the answer was *Choco Zoenen*. But they are now simply called '*Zoenen*.' No shame, no blame. Just change the name.

The supermarket chain Albert Heijn started making their own version of the cookie, which they chose to call '*Negen Zoete*' Kisses. It's clearly not *Neger Zoenen* – that would be offensive! …But it's enough like *Neger Zoenen* to appeal to all those die-hard racists out there. Like Geert Wilders.

CHAPTER 14

DUTCH STANDARDS

It is tempting to make fun of Dutch '*gekke gewoontes*' (silly standards or habits). Yet they can make more sense than what you're used to.

QUESTION 1

What is the proper term for your relationship partner, when you've decided to do *samenwonen* (living together) instead of getting married?

A Girlfriend

B Wife

C Baby Mama

ANSWER = NONE OF THE ABOVE

As of this writing, Dutch society still hasn't come up with a decent term for 'significant other.' I've met too many Dutch men my age, who still don't know how to refer to the female partner they've been living with for 10 years.

"This is my... girlfriend."

"How long have you been dating?"

"We're not dating; we live together. She's like my wife."

"How long have you been married?"

"We're not married... she's my partner."

"So you're in business?"

"We're not in business. She's my... baby mama?"

Dutch folks, you invented the term *samenwonen*. You really should figure out what to call the person you're spending your life with. In many cases, why not just say *samenwoman*?

QUESTION 2

How many of the following definitions could apply to the term *gas station*?

A A place to put gasoline in your car

B A place to put natural gas in your car

C A place where the food will give you gas

ANSWER = ALL OF THE ABOVE

The term 'gas station' is terribly unspecific. The Dutch have 'tank stations,' which is only confusing if you're driving a tank.

QUESTION 3

When does a Dutch person give you their cell number?

A When they live in a prison cell

B When they are a monk

C When they have been living in the United States

ANSWER = C

Americans have 'cell numbers' because they have 'cellular' phones. Dutch people will give you a 'mobile' number, because they have the much more sensibly named 'mobile phones.' It could be worse: the term for a German mobile phone is a 'Handy,' which only succeeds in making me giggle inappropriately. Giving someone your *cell number* should only mean one thing: you are in prison. Or perhaps you are a bee.

Of course, it can be confusing when you get caught in between cultures. If this happens, remember to just relax and 'go your gang.'

CHAPTER 15
DUTCH CUISINE

On the international stage, cuisine can play a pivotal role. Compare the climate summits in 2009 and 2015. In Copenhagen 2009, the Danish Environmental Minister had a simple strategy: lock the delegates in a room and don't let them out until they reach a deal. There was no deal. In 2015, the French hosts stopped the whole summit to make sure everyone had enough to eat and drink, providing breaks for coffee, croissants and chocolate. The result was the Paris Climate Accord.

QUESTION 1

What did the Dutch serve European leaders at the 2016 kickoff of Nederland hosting the European Presidency?

A Cheese blocks and mustard
B Herring and smoked eel
C Coffee and mini muffins

ANSWER = A & C

For the first half of 2016, the Dutch played host to the EU Presidency. One of the stated policy goals was to avoid wasteful spending. Hence, the afternoon session featured coffee and mini muffins, and the evening session reportedly welcomed dignitaries with cheese blocks and mustard.

Rumor has it that there was also warm food. This probably means the Dutch delicacy known as 'bitter balls,' which is not a description of flavor as much as a way to describe how foreign dignitaries feel when presented with deep fried gravy. The deep-fried exterior of bitter balls will mask the scalding-hot inside, so that one can hardly take a bite without burning one's tongue within the first 30 seconds. After that, the Dutch hosts can serve any number of follow-ups from liverwurst to pickled onions and describe them as delicious. And the guests will have no choice but to take their word for it.

QUESTION 2

What does FEBO stand for?

A *Frans & Eefje's Borrel Hapjes*

B Ferdinand Bolstraat

C Freshly Embalmed Bovine Offal

ANSWER = B

FEBO takes its name from its first-ever location on Ferdinand Bolstraat. Specifically, they took the FE from Ferdinand and the BO from Bolstraat. If they wanted to be more accurate, they could have just added two more letters and called their place 'FER BOL.' Because the inside of a *kroket* looks a lot like something a cat coughed up.

QUESTION 3

How can you tell when you've truly assimilated into Dutch culture?

A When your mashed potato *stamppot* satisfies a Dutch family

B When you really appreciate a cheese sandwich

C When you spill chocolate sprinkles all over the floor and still scoop them and eat them, knowing chocolate sprinkles are indistinguishable from mouse poops

ANSWER = ALL OF THE ABOVE

My wife is Dutch, and my *stamppot* is good enough that she has asked me to make it more than once. As for option C, yes, I've done that. And as for option B, I do a lot of corporate speaking, and the stereotypes about Dutch lunches are true. I've frequently encountered the traditional sad raft of floppy Dutch *broodjes*: one with meat; one with cheese; one with egg and one with vegetables. My American colleagues will tear apart several of these *broodjes* to make one 'proper' sandwich, with meat and cheese and egg together. But then one day we got an upgrade: the bread was proper bakery bread, and the cheese was Dutch aged cheese. My American colleagues went to pull the *broodjes* apart, and I said, "No! This is a true *Broodje Oude Kaas*." That's when my colleagues told me, "Yeah, you're really Dutch now."

One day, with my lunch, I may even want to drink a tall glass of *karnemelk* (buttermilk). But I predict that level of Dutchness will never come.

CHAPTER 16
DUTCH GROUP BEHAVIOR

Dutch people are famous for having a very open and tolerant society. The good news is: you can relax and be yourself. The bad news is: if being yourself is not Dutch enough, they'll simply laugh in your face. Because they're also 'just being themselves.'

QUESTION 1

Which is more important?

A *Doe Normaal,* 'Do Normal'

B *Doe Maar Gewoon,* 'Just act normal'

ANSWER = BOTH

Remember, Dutch society is known for being open and tolerant. So, their version of 'Do Normal' can seem rather weird. To the Dutch mind, the only thing weird is trying to pretend you're not weird. In practice, there's a big difference between the written and the spoken 'Doe Normaal.' When you see 'Doe Normaal' in writing, it's generally in the context of Dutch tolerance. When a Dutch person *says* 'Doe Normaal,' it means they're not being tolerant at all, and you should change your behavior immediately.

'*Doe maar gewoon*' also translates to 'just act normal.' But it has a follow-up: '*Doe maar gewoon; je bent al gek genoeg.*' Literally, 'Just be yourself. You're crazy enough as it is.' Yes, Dutch folks have a history of being tolerant. As such, they've seen it all before, and your version of 'crazy' is not so much shocking as 'probably annoying.' A building that looks like an enormous bathtub? That's just Dutch architecture. A man and a woman with their genitals pierced together? That's just a poster for a nightclub. A guy in a gold G-string dangling over your table while you're trying to order a drink? That's every Friday at Leidseplein. Just act normal.

QUESTION 2

The Netherlands is a country that values the right to privacy. You are in public and someone is eating. What do you do?

A Nod politely as you pass

B Get something to eat yourself

C Respect their privacy

ANSWER = NONE OF THE ABOVE

While most social interactions are dictated by the 'Doe Normaal' rule, according to which you act as if whatever is going on is perfectly normal, there is an exception when someone is eating in public. Then it is important to stare at them, point at them and say, "*Eet smakelijk*" (*Bon appétit*) as loudly as possible, until they choke on their food.

QUESTION 3

You are in a queue at a public event and someone sneaks to the front. What do you do?

A Look the other way. Pointing only makes it worse

B Politely point out that there is a line

C Pretend like you know the person and also sneak to the front

ANSWER = NONE OF THE ABOVE

The correct answer is:
Act like you've never heard of the concept of queuing and – if there are train doors involved – attempt to trample the slow and the weak.

CHAPTER 17

DUTCH CHEAPNESS

Another stereotype about the Dutch is that they're cheap. They're certainly stingy with their love for bailing out the rest of Europe.

QUESTION 1

Where are Dutch people the least cheap?

A Flevoland

B Limburg

C Noord Holland

ANSWER = B

In the part of the Netherlands known as 'below the rivers,' people are known as more generous (with the exception of one very guarded politician from Venlo). My mother in-law lives on the border with Limburg, which is known for its fruit pie *vlaai*. Every time we go to visit, she'll serve a plate of *vlaai*, a cup of coffee, and then a cookie from the tin. More than once I've spilled the coffee, trying to balance this bounty of items. Wiping scalding hot coffee off my lap, I've sometimes wished for *less* generosity.

And let's not forget the generosity of the Dutch government – for those who seek a tax haven. On the one hand, the Dutch Prime Minister is known for saying that Southern Europeans must pay their taxes. On the other hand, if they would register themselves as corporations in the Netherlands, they could get away with paying no taxes at all.

QUESTION 2

Which term best describes Dutch cheapness?

A Frugal

B Reserved

C Stingy

ANSWER = A & C

But are the Dutch really cheap? Or are they more *zuinig*, which translates to somewhere between *frugal* and *stingy*. There's a reason so many Dutch businesses are into W2R (Waste to Resource). Case in point, they love TLAs (Three-Letter Acronyms). Such as UCO (Used Cooking Oil): Dutch startup SkyNRG is recycling cooking oil to make jet fuel. Now, your next flight on KLM might be powered by LNF: Last Night's *Frites*.

Or CNG (Compressed Natural Gas): In Friesland, waste management company Omrin recycles and composts enough organic waste to have enough CNG to power their entire fleet of trucks – and have enough left over to add to the national gas grid. I asked the CEO, "Why isn't everyone doing this?" And he said, "Well, Groningen still has a lot of natural gas. I guess they like earthquakes?"

QUESTION 3

Which of the following public artworks typifies Dutch cheapness?

A

B

C

ANSWER = NONE OF THE ABOVE

The first sculpture is a series of metal tree trunks, located in a forest in Amsterdam. At some point, the city must have had a sack of money to plant some new trees, perhaps in an area that needed more trees. But no – instead, there was an artist who said, "I have an idea! Why not make people think about *dead* trees?" Less green, more death. If you can afford to think this way, you're not exactly cheap.

The second sculpture stands in front of an Amsterdam school. It's a sculpture of a man. How can you tell it's a man? Because of the huge, spiky steel erection. Necessary? No. Welcome? Probably not. But still funded with public money.

The third sculpture was commissioned for the opening of a public building in Amsterdam *Oud West*. Integrated into the façade of the building is a series of white ladders extending up and out and high above the street. At the top of the ladders is a life-size human figure with its arms stretched up to the heavens. And it's called *How to Meet an Angel*. What is the public building that received such a sculpture? It's a mental health center for people with psychiatric problems.

If the Dutch can afford public art like this, then you can't call the Dutch cheap.

CHAPTER 18
DUTCH LANGUAGE

In Dutch you can come so close to making sense... and then there's that one false word or sound that throws everything off. For example, when you sit down to eat, and you want to say, "*Eet smakelijk,*" make sure you use the long *a* sound. Otherwise you've said, "Chew with your mouth open."

QUESTION 1

When you tell a fellow passenger in a train compartment you'd be happy to switch seats with them to ride facing backwards, you say, "*Ik kan achterop rijden.*" What have you actually said?

A I'll ride backwards
B I'll ride on the back
C I'll ride on your back

ANSWER = B

The word you were looking for is *achteruit.* But enjoy as everyone in the train compartment has a good laugh picturing you being dragged to your death behind the train.

QUESTION 2

When referring to a decision by the school board, you say, "*De beslissing is ongesteld.*" What have you actually said?

A The decision is mentally unstable
B The decision is being digested
C The decision is menstruating

ANSWER = C

The word you were looking for is *uitgesteld*. Most Dutch people will know which word you were looking for. And they will still look at you with incomprehension and contempt.

QUESTION 3

When a group of orange-clad boys are playing football on the day of a big match for the Dutch World Cup team, you say, "*Wat is je voorspel door vanavond?*" What have you actually said?

A What is your prediction for tonight?
B What is your foreplay for tonight?
C What is your ball game tonight?

ANSWER = B

The word you were looking for is *voorspelling*. Instead, you're now the guy who goes up to kids on a playground and asks them about their sexual plans for later.

CHAPTER 19
DUTCH ENVIRONMENT

There's no shortage of climate innovation in the Netherlands – as long as you don't look at the government. Rotterdam designer Daan Roosegarde invented a smog magnet to remove air pollution. Towns like Uitgeest are creating the first-ever solar bike path. And as for the Dutch government at the time of this writing – they are doing so little to meet their own environmental goals that they were successfully sued by the Dutch group Urgenda, creating a worldwide precedent. So technically, yes the Dutch government helped environmental innovation – just not in the way they intended.

QUESTION 1

Which phrase best describes the modern Dutch attitude toward growth?

A Full is Full

B The polder model

C 'On the eighth day, the Dutch made Holland'

ANSWER = A

Yes, Dutch history is all about draining water and creating land, or *polder*. You might think that – for a country that created much of its landmass using shovels and pumps – they'd be proud of their history of cooperation, known as 'The Polder Model.' But lately, it's more common to see 'the Polder Model is dead.'

Perhaps its Dutch modesty that resists taking too much credit for their engineering successes. Look at Flevoland. Just 100 years ago, it was mostly underwater. Now it's an entire new province! The rest of world looked at the new Dutch map and said, “It’s a miracle!” But ask most Dutch people about Flevoland, and the general response is, “Mwah, it’s okay, but I wouldn’t want to live there… It’s not *gezellig*.”

It was in Flevoland that the PVV party – known for saying, “Full is Full” – gained a majority in the city council of the capital, Almere. Yet, it’s a bit odd to say, “Full is full” in a city whose land didn’t exist 100 years ago. If you ever hear Dutch people say, “Full is full,” you may remind them: “You’re Dutch! Just make more land.”

QUESTION 2

Which of the following is NOT true?

A 26% of the Netherlands is under sea level

B Nederland is the 3rd biggest agricultural exporter in the world

C 22% of the world’s potatoes originate in Nederland

ANSWER = B

Actually, tiny Nederland is the world’s SECOND biggest agricultural exporter, by value. Impossible as it may seem, a 2014 report from the University of Wageningen reported that Dutch exports of dairy, eggs, meat, flowers, fruit and vegetables are second only to the United States. It’s truly ‘America First, the Netherlands Second.’

The Netherlands boasts 10,000 hectares of greenhouses. The Dutch are responsible for 22% of the world’s exported potatoes. And according to Oxfam, the Netherlands is the world’s number one country for plentiful, affordable food. How can this be?

According to *The Economist,* the Dutch secret is ‘sustainable and intensive food production,’ including innovations such as fermenting their hay. Fermented hay makes a big difference in cow poop. Mucking out the cowshed has been a Herculean task, ever since the Augean stables of Greek mythology. But by fermenting their hay, Dutch farms create liquid manure, which is removed by – yes – water. It’s apparently a game changer. The process of fermenting hay is so efficient that there's enough manure left over to create biogas to heat Dutch homes. Leave it to the inventors of the poop shelf to pioneer cow poop innovation.

QUESTION 3

Which of the following natural disasters resulted in help from the Dutch?

A Hurricane Sandy

B Hurricane Ivan

C Hurricane Katrina

ANSWER = A & C

First came Hurricane Katrina in 2005, when Dutch expertise was called in to clean up the mess in Louisiana and help prevent another mess. A Dutch friend of mine works in Chicago, and he helped connect the Dutch engineering firm Royal Haskoning with the US Army Corps of Engineers. Up to that point, the US Army had been famous for its engineering of a shipping canal from the Mississippi river to the Gulf of Mexico. It was the Dutch who pointed out that the canal also acted as an enormous storm funnel aimed directly at downtown New Orleans. Royal Haskoning are now helping build storm barriers to prevent another Hurricane Katrina. But they reportedly didn't want to make a big deal about it, because that would be bragging, aka *opscheppen*.

Next came Hurricane Sandy in New York, 2012. Again, America invited the Dutch to advise. Specifically, they asked Henk Ovink from the Dutch Water Management Ministry *Rijkswaterstaat*. I did an interview with Ovink, who reported that the Obama Administration was proud to show what they'd learned from New Orleans. They had built a breakwater so that any storm surge aimed at Manhattan would be deflected – towards New Jersey. Thinking holistically, Ovink asked, "How does New Jersey feel about that?" The New Yorkers reportedly replied, "Forget about it!" The Dutch still have some work to do.

CHAPTER 20

DUTCH POLITICS

Especially if you're comparing to America, Dutch politics can seem like Alice *Through the Looking Glass*. Liberals are Conservative. Socialists are Republican, and the whole thing seems mad as a hatter.

QUESTION 1

How many different political parties are there in a Dutch election?

A Just enough

B Not enough

C Too many to comprehend

ANSWER = C

The Netherlands is a country with 17 million people – and about 17 million different political parties. Voting in the Netherlands is like ordering from a tapas menu. So many choices! And, of course, you're tempted to try a little bit from this one, and a little bit from that one. Which is why it's unfortunate that you can only vote for one thing. (But have faith – by the time the coalition negotiations are over – you're guaranteed to end up with more than one item on the table.)

Every time there's an election, there are 10 parties you know, another 10 that never make it into parliament, and sometimes another 10 parties that have never existed before – and may never exist again. Dutch people really like their parties. Some of them are like the Unity Party in Almere, which was founded by just two guys, with the mission to create more unity. Two years later, they split up because they couldn't agree on the proper definition of *unity*. Then they formed their own parties and had to fight over which party would keep the name 'Unity.' That's why there are so many political parties. The smaller the country, the more they like to disagree.

QUESTION 2

According to most Dutch people, how are mayors appointed?

A Elected by the city council
B Appointed by the King
C Appointed by the Cabinet
D Direct election

ANSWER = EVERYTHING EXCEPT D

First, the King's Commissioner gets to pre-select a list of candidates. Then the candidates are reviewed by the city council's (secret) committee. Then they send their choice to the Cabinet's Minister of the Interior to be appointed. If you want to be entertained, ask any two Dutch people to explain this process and watch them argue, as they come nowhere near the right answer. The only thing of which everyone is certain: it's not D.

QUESTION 3

Who reads the annual *Prinsjesdag* speech to the nation?

A The Prince
B The King
C The Prime Minister

ANSWER = B

Prinsjesdag is Prince's Day, which occurs every September and involves a speech read by a man who's not a prince. The speech is written by the Prime Minister, and not the King. The day begins with the King riding in his golden coach through the streets of the capital – which is not really the capital. And the golden coach is no longer golden. All of this is so that the Finance Minister can stand in front of Parliament and say, "Look at me and my million euro note!"

CHAPTER 21

DUTCH HEALTH CARE

As Westley says in *Princess Bride,* "Life is pain. Anyone who says otherwise is trying to sell you something."

QUESTION 1

Which of the following questions has appeared in the Dutch Assimilation Exam?

A 'You've just had your fourth baby. How many more babies is it healthy to have?'

B 'Your neighbors just placed a wooden stork in their front yard. Should you politely inform them where babies really come from?'

C 'How long after a miscarriage does a woman resume menstruation?'

ANSWER = C

The Dutch author Rodaan Al Galidi reported seeing the question about miscarriage in his assimilation course, and it was corroborated by the examiners. I think anyone receiving this question on the exam should be able to submit a rebuttal question: "What's this got to do with cultural assimilation?" If this question is on the assimilation exam, then somewhere there must be a medical school gynecologists' exam asking, 'Who painted *The Nightwatch*?'

QUESTION 2

Which of the following is an acceptable way to show annoyance with another person?

A 'Go get cholera'
B 'Go get typhoid fever'
C 'Go get cancer'

ANSWER = ALL OF THE ABOVE

Dutch culture prides itself on its directness. In medicine, the same Dutch directness applies.

It starts with Dutch insults, which go medical right away. In English-speaking countries, one of the worst things you can say is, "F**k off," which basically means 'Go give yourself an orgasm,' which is comparatively quite polite.

QUESTION 3

If you ask your doctor for a local anesthetic during an operation, what response can you expect?
A "Don't worry. The pain will be quick"
B "I won't lie. This is going to hurt"
C "Pain is part of life"

ANSWER = ALL OF THE ABOVE

Dutch society deserves its reputation for being tolerant. This includes a rather high tolerance for pain – as anyone who's visited the Dutch health care system will know. In other countries, you may encounter the phrase "This might hurt a bit," and it might hurt – a bit. Dutch health care professionals are more direct. They don't sugar-coat it. You will hear, "This is going to hurt." And oh, it hurts.

In America, you can't get through a check-out line without being offered three different kinds of ibuprofen. In the Netherlands, if you try to buy ibuprofen, you get a small interrogation: "Are you aware what you're purchasing? Are you familiar with the workings of this drug? Have you considered the potential effects?" Yes. The effects of painkillers are to kill pain. But at the Dutch pharmacy they look at you like you might be a drug addict.

Some countries believe a positive mental attitude can boost your health. Dutch research seems to have concluded: it's better to admit suffering is inevitable. If you ask for a painkiller, you will either be told, "Don't worry, it'll be quick." Or you will even be teased for being weak. "LIFE IS PAIN," your doctor will say, not content to torture just your body, but also your naive worldview.

CHAPTER 22
DUTCH SERVICE

The term 'Dutch service' can be an oxymoron. In the Netherlands, 'The client is king (just not the boss).'

QUESTION 1

Which of the following is a Dutch waiter most likely to say?

A "You're right, your dish isn't cooked properly. I'll have the kitchen fix it"
B "Are you feeling cold? I can turn up the heat"
C "Thank you for holding the door open while I carry this tray"

ANSWER = NONE OF THE ABOVE

The correct answers would be:

A "The kitchen makes no mistakes. Your dish is supposed to taste that way"
B "Why would I turn up the heat? I feel fine"
C "Why are you holding the door open for me? I'm not going to sleep with you" (actual quote)

QUESTION 2

What is the meaning of '*Heeft het gesmaakt?*'

A Did you make this yourself?
B Did it taste good?
C Did it smack you?

ANSWER = B

More and more, it is possible to hear the phrase: 'How is your meal' *before* the end of the meal. But mostly the server will come after the meal and ask, "*Heeft het gesmaakt?*" This means: 'Did it taste good?' But it really means: 'I hope you're done, because I'm taking your plate.' For fun, you can tell them the food was not perfect and maybe even give them a message for the kitchen, such as "Too much salt." And then you can watch your server stand there malfunctioning, until you get your line right: "You're supposed to say: 'It was *lekker*.'"

QUESTION 3

Which is the most *gezellig*?

A A sociable place to hang out
B A sociable place to work
C A sociable place where workers hang out

ANSWER = C

On a sunny day in Amsterdam, it's lovely to see the café terraces fill up in an instant. Everyone is drinking and soaking up the sun. And there's probably someone smoking right next to you. And you can't actually get a drink. Because the one next to you with the cigarette is your waiter. Shouldn't they be serving drinks? "Nah, we're just being *gezellig*."

America is known as a land of rugged 'do-it-yourself' types. But in fact, it's America where you're bombarded with "Can I help you?" And in the Netherlands, when you want to order, you're on your own.

CHAPTER 23

DUTCH BIKES PART 2

Since so many Dutch people ride a bicycle every day, the need for Dutch mandatory biking lessons is imperative. And since the Netherlands will never let that happen, here is second set of questions on biking etiquette.

QUESTION 1

While biking, you come upon a sign saying 'Detour. Biking further will bring a € 50 penalty,' what do you do?

A Ignore the sign. Bike further

B Follow the detour

C Take a completely different route

ANSWER = B & C

While some cyclists will ignore the sign (and rarely provide me the satisfaction of then being stopped by police), most cyclists will indeed deviate. I do too. Usually halfway through the detour I'll have come up with a totally new route, and I'll take that one. There's also the option of getting off your bike and walking through the road construction, but you run the risk of being run over – and laughed at – by the cyclists who ignore the sign.

QUESTION 2

When biking in a roundabout, what hand signal do Dutch people give upon exiting?

A None

B Half-mast hand signal

C Full hand signal for bikes, cars and trams to see

ANSWER = B

The common-sense answer would be C. But to be truly Dutch, it's B. This answer takes into account the rules of the Dutch driving exam, which is divided into 'Theory' and 'Practical.' In Theory, yes you're supposed signal when you turn, high enough so everyone can see, and you won't get run over. In Practice, Dutch people signal, but not too overtly, as that would be uncool. The Dutch way to signal is to look as if you have a muscle disorder and can barely raise your arm.

QUESTION 3

The Netherlands is a country of bicycles. Biking etiquette is very important. You are on a bike path, and you come across someone biking the wrong way. It is someone you recognize. What is the most Dutch reaction?

A Wave but do not stop
B Wave, stop and talk on the sidewalk
C Tease your friend for going the wrong way

ANSWER = NONE OF THE ABOVE

If you want to be truly Dutch, the correct answer is: both of you stop in the middle of the bike path and chat for as long as possible while everyone else crashes into each other trying not to hit you.

CHAPTER 24
DUTCH BIKE PATHS

Surely, a system of quality bike paths must be considered a pinnacle of civilization. In the Netherlands, there are many bike paths. Other countries have bike paths as well – but they're still adjusting to the concept. In the United States, I once saw a road sign saying 'Give space to bikes' – located in the bike path.

QUESTION 1

What is the most annoying vehicle on the Dutch bike path?

A Scooter

B Scooter

C Scooter

ANSWER = SCOOTER

The Dutch government introduced a new law on 8 April 2019: No more scooters on the bike path. Unfortunately, most scooter riders assume the new law was issued on 1 April, and they treat it like an April Fools' joke.

There's a reason the Italians named their Vespa scooters after the wasp: they're supremely annoying. The scooter is also an expert-level example of Dutch assimilation. If you complain about them too loudly, you sound like a spoiled expat. The challenge is to do like the natives and tolerate them.

QUESTION 2

Which color license plate means a scooter is allowed to ride on the bike path?

A Yellow
B Blue
C NONE

ANSWER = C

Before 2019, yellow number plates meant a scooter was required to ride in the street, and blue number plates meant a scooter could ride on the bike path. As it has been explained to me, the blue plate exemption was introduced in the 1960s to accommodate women whose hair styles were getting crushed by their helmets. So not only are blue plate scooters violating the law – and polluting the bike path with their exhaust – they are also inherently sexist.

Since 2019, scooters with blue number plates are technically required to change to yellow and ride in the street. In practice, the blue number plate scooters started riding on the street, on the bike path, on the sidewalk, and over your bike if you say anything about it.

QUESTION 3

You are biking on a bike path marked 'No Motor Scooters,' when you encounter a motor scooter. What should you do?

A Take no notice and wait for the police to take action
B Roll your eyes and congratulate yourself for being tolerant
C Make contact with the scooter and point to the 'No Motor Scooter' signs

ANSWER = B

Waiting for the police to take action is not an option, as that will never happen. Granted – with a simple traffic control – the police could rake in thousands of euros per week. Or the police could simply install a speeding camera Dutch invention, after all – and make millions. But as of this writing, Dutch police are happy just to spend money putting up the signs – and leaving it at that.

The most common Dutch reaction is to roll one's eyes, make a rude gesture, and carry on. But hey, if you should happen to make contact with a scooter, and you're tempted to point to the 'No Motor Scooter' signs, you can also take the opportunity to whack them on the head and say, "You could have avoided that whack, if you'd worn a helmet, in the street."

CHAPTER 25

DUTCH LANGUAGE PART 2

Speaking Dutch among Dutch people is rather like giving a toast while drunk. You know you're going to humiliate yourself, but you do it anyway. Here are some tips to survive.

QUESTION 1

Which is the correct meaning of the term *Hè hè?*

A This is nice

B How hard was that!?

C Oh, well

ANSWER = ALL OF THE ABOVE

There are many need-to-know definitions of the term '*hè hè*,' none of which are covered in the Dutch language textbook.

Definition A is when you walk outside after a week of rain, and suddenly the sun is shining. Here you are allowed to say '*hè hè*,', as in 'nice weather,' with the unspoken subtext '*...finally*.'

Definition B is used when someone finally succeeds at a task that should be easy. An example would be during penalty kicks for the Dutch national football team.

(For those who don't follow football, or call it 'soccer,' penalty kicks work like this: a bunch of guys kick a ball around for two whole hours, but no one scores. That's when the referee takes the ball, puts it right in front of the net and says, "See if you can kick it in now.")

When the Dutch national team finally scores during a penalty kick, the proper reaction is "HÈ HÈ!?" (*How hard was that?!*)

Definition C is when the Dutch national team inevitably lose on penalty kicks and are again eliminated. Then the proper reaction is a series of nonsense syllables, followed by "*hè hè.*" Such as: "*Nee, joh! O, Sjonge jonge jonge jonge! Kut met peren! God verdikkie... ahh... hè hè.*"

QUESTION 2

Which of the following is not a real Dutch name?

A Freek

B Joke

C Floor Sander

D Fokko

E Sikko

ANSWER = C

In the Netherlands there are men named *Freek* and women named *Joke*. The name *Floor* is a real Dutch name, as is *Sander*. But I haven't yet met a 'Floor Sander.' I was once at a business meeting where I was introduced to two clients named Fokko and Sikko. I had to ask, "Is this a joke?" They said, "No, Joke is back at the office."

QUESTION 3

Which of the following is a Dutch word?

A *Landje*

B *Planeetje*

C *Zonnetje*

ANSWER = ALL OF THE ABOVE

When in doubt, you can put a diminutive suffix on anything. Yes, you can look for a sizable house, but it's best to refer to it as a *huis-je*. Having acquired the house, it is customary to acquire a tree: *boom-pje*. And a pet: *beest-je*.

What does it say about Dutch culture? Maybe it has something to do with growing up next to a big sibling like Germany. Some people call it an inferiority complex. Some say it's those Calvinist roots, demanding modesty in all things. But that's not quite it. While some cultures – say America's – like to 'Think Big,' the Dutch language forces you to celebrate scaling down. An entire country can be referred to as a *land-je*. And it's quite common to hear Dutch people refer to the sun – *zon* – with a diminutive. The largest object in the solar system, and the Dutch call it *zonnetje*. What could be more Dutch?

25 MOST INAPPROPRIATE DUTCH SIGNS

Afuk.

The Frisian language center. Where they give Afuk.

Bad Hotel.

Zero Stars.

The BARF Menu.

So nice your dog will eat it twice.

The shop is called 'Black for Kids.'

...But the sign clearly says 'Black Kids for Sale Sale Sale.'

Himalaya Sushi Bar.

The Himalayas – nowhere near the ocean.
"But our fishing lines are really long."

Bribus Extra.

"If you're going to bribe us, why not bribe us extra?"

Closed.

This store is always Closed.

Dick Kok.

"Gather round, kids! It's the Dick Kok wagon!"

Dogstyle.
Yes, the owner does know what
it means in English.

Down Under Hair.
Hair styling for those hard-to-reach areas.

Firezone.

"Want to blow up your car while refueling?
Come on down to Firezone!"

Café FUKU.

Always the most authentic Dutch service.

Gencydo Neusspray.
When you want to kill every last living thing in your nose.

Spotted by my publisher in front of the sign, saying 'Black Kids for Sale.'
What better place to put on blackface?

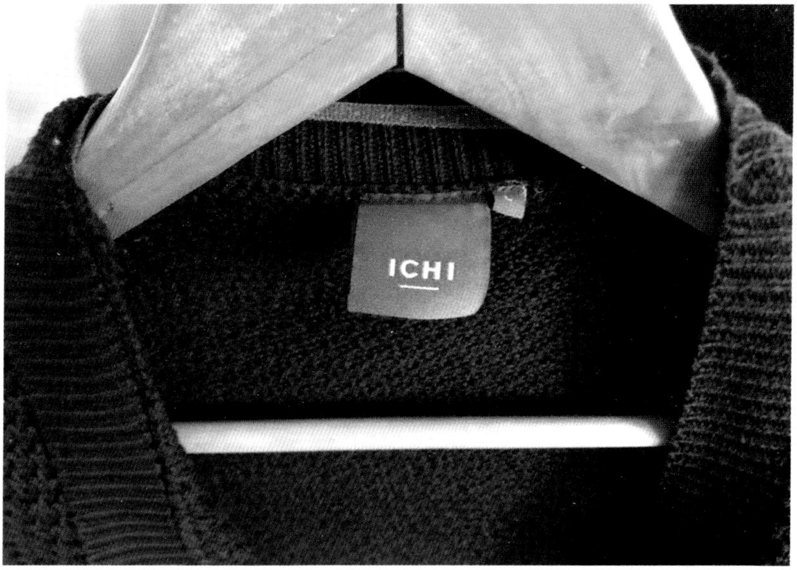

Ichi Sweater.
Guaranteed itchy.

"The name of your company is Kronenburg Group.
What logo would you like?" "KKK, please!"

Mild Doux.
Pronounced 'mildew.' For that authentic mildew smell.

Notities.
You can draw whatever you want in this blank notebook. But please Notities.

Puspita.
You'll never want to eat food again.

Royal-Douche.
This contractor is more than a huge pain –
he's a Royal Douche.

Lies.

"Welcome to the Town of Lies! Population 800 million!"

Ufuk Shoarma.

Oh no, you didn't.

Vague Coiffures.
Really unspecific hair care.

Wang Flavour.
He's not just pulling your wang.

SP SENATOR TINY KOX

Tiny Kox (1953, Zeelst) acquired degrees in Eersel (1970) and Eindhoven (1973), and afterwards received a law degree at the University of Tilburg (1975), where he has lived since 1973. From 1978 to 1982 he was active as the coordinator of the Tilburg legal aid centre. In 1978 he became editor of the *Buurtkrant*, an activist housing bulletin published by the SP, of which he had become a member in 1975.

Tiny Kox. His name is *Martinus*.

He could've chosen Martin. Or Marty. But no: *Tiny*.

THE AUTHOR

Gregory Shapiro – the American Netherlander – spent the first 25 years of his life in the United States and the next 25 in the Netherlands. He arrived in 1994 to take a job with the Boom Chicago comedy theater – for just one summer. But as he discovered, the Dutch can be addictive. Shapiro came for work and stayed for love. After ten years of practicing his awful Dutch language skills, he completed the equivalent of a Dutch citizenship course and achieved dual citizenship – meaning he no longer feels 100% at home anywhere on the planet.

Shapiro celebrates his split nationalities with a master class in cultural assimilation, known as 'Culture Shock Therapy.' He has performed at corporate events for the King of the Netherlands, for the French President, for NATO, and once in the Business Class section of a KLM 747.

Shapiro lives in Amsterdam with his wife, who is an artist and writer. Together, they have two bilingual children and a black Labrador, who will lick you if she gets the chance. Shapiro is incredibly handsome and professional – and talks about himself in the third person.

Photo Adrie Mouthaan